COMPASSION IN COMMERCE

First published by Asherah Books, 2019

A CIP catalogue record for this book is available from the British Library.

ISBN: 978-1-909187-96-2

COMPASSION IN COMMERCE

Cher Chevalier
Judith Clegg

Asherah Books
London

CONTENTS

INTRODUCTION

Compassion in Commerce covers key aspects of how business affects our world in all areas from Dedicated Diversity to Compassion Challenges, Kind Food, Compassionate Communication and Modern Models to success through Acme, Skill-Sets, Robotics, Universal Basic Income, Excellent Futures for All and Giving Back.

As we find ourselves having contributed to the impending environmental crisis, with scientists warning that we have only a decade to prevent global warming from increasing beyond 1.5C, we must ask ourselves if we are prepared to go on as caretakers, or as killers of our planet, and whether our world and humanity itself can survive and evolve without compassion in commerce?

Through business, we have the power to create good change, meaningful work, a fair income for citizens to provide for themselves and their loved ones, the route to excellent health and wellbeing for all, as well as a sustainable future for our earth and its inhabitants.

Looking to the end result of commerce it is vital to understand for what we are aiming to build our ventures. What is our motive? To be rich? To change the world? To secure a future for our family? To fix something we think is broken in our economy or society? To give all of our money away to help others? At this juncture in human evolution, we need to act now, with compassion and conscience, to ensure that our planet not only survives, but thrives for future generations.

Make no mistake, whatever each of us builds will leave an indelible mark, so our responsibility as world shapers needs to be to build a good legacy, and one that is both helpful and harmless.

Just as diversity underpins the circle of life so too it drives the wheel of business. Companies with more diverse teams including gender, racial

1

and ethnic diversity are significantly more successful, and profitable; and we would argue that compassionate visionaries are the pioneers of true success.

Each of us is blessed with unique skill-sets. When these are given the freedom to flourish and flow, miracles can happen. Together, our capacity for good works is limitless!

"We believe that the secrets to success are hard work, kindness, honesty, imagination, and going the extra mile. So, with noble goals, we humbly invite you to join us in embracing a compassionate vision and discovering simple yet mighty ways we can improve our world for the benefit of all beings." Cher & Judith

Cher Chevalier is a world-renowned Spiritual Adviser, Co-Author of Meditations that launched Calm, iTunes App of The Year 2017, Co-Creator of PAWS - The Policy for Animal Welfare Scheme, Writer and Co-Creator of The Compassion In Commerce Training Program, Co-Creator of The #HANDSOFF Campaign, Co-Writer of the "LOST CHILD" Song, Founder and CEO of Animals Actually Ltd, and Author of the following 31 books: INNER JOURNEY MEDITATIONS with Cher Chevalier & Liz Solari, The Hidden Secrets of a MODERN SEER, The Hidden Truths of a MODERN SEER, The Hidden Life of a MODERN SEER, SLIM: Step Lightly In Mind, Body, Spirit, and ANIMALS ACTUALLY A-Z.

Cher was born in England into a family that boasts four generations of vegetarians and vegans. She endured near-death experiences in childhood, after which her psychic and mystical experiences began. Cher has worked as a Spiritual Adviser for over 25 years, appeared on many mainstream TV shows; including Celebrity World Cup Soccer Six where she performed absent healing for footballer Wayne Rooney, live on Sky One. She has been featured in numerous publications and radio shows around the globe. Cher was the Spiritual Adviser on the UNLOCKED movie; she was also hired to help launch the Matt Damon/Clint Eastwood movie HEREAFTER. Cher leads a devotional life.

Judith Clegg is a serial entrepreneur; Co-Creator of PAWS - The Policy for Animal Welfare Scheme, Writer and Co-Creator of The Compassion In Commerce Training Program, Co-Creator of The #HANDSOFF Campaign, and Founder of London and New York based innovation agency, Takeout, which works with organisations to help them innovate, create new flagship products, services, revenues and profits.

Judith previously founded Glasshouse, an organisation that provides support, inspiration and networks for entrepreneurs, investors and digital innovators; and was a co-founder of Moonfruit, an early pioneer of social networking, acquired by Yell. She is a trustee of Police Now, a UK charity with a mission to transform communities, reduce crime and increase the public's confidence in policing. Having a passion for tech, Judith has been listed as one of the Top Digital Powerbrokers in the UK by Wired Magazine; as one of the Top 50 Most Influential Britons in Technology (Daily Telegraph); a Global Top 50 Women to Watch in Technology (Femmeonomics); finalist for Cosmopolitan Woman of the Year; one of WIE's 50 Global Exceptional Women, and has been listed as one of Inspiring Fifty's most inspirational EU women in Tech.

CHAPTER 1
COMPASSION IN COMMERCE

COMPASSION IN COMMERCE

Principles

The ultimate business goal is to aim for the very highest, the point at which something is at its very best. Acme.

Real business success is for the benefit of ALL beings. For example, giving a woman in Africa a high-powered technology job helps all around her and can change society's attitudes; or consider the rapid success of plant-based foods which are kind to animals, the planet and people.

Through business we have the power to create meaningful work, a fair income for citizens to provide for their life and loved ones, access to excellent health and wellbeing for all and a sustainable future for the earth.

Delivering peace and prosperity through commerce is a blueprint for success.

The future of success has to be good. In the not too distant future, you will only be considered cool or get famous if you are good - good for business, good for consumers, good for the planet, and good for animals.

In our experience, the best, most successful and happiest business people are those motivated by uplifting others and making the world a better, kinder place.

The root meaning of the word commerce (the exchange of goods and services) made its way into the English language from the Latin word commercium - meaning "together."

But we find ourselves having contributed to the impending environmental crisis, with scientists warning that we have only a decade to prevent global warming from increasing beyond 1.5C, and must ask ourselves if we are prepared to go on as caretakers, or as killers of our planet, and whether our world and humanity itself can survive and evolve without compassion in commerce?

With the UN reporting that:

- 783 million people live below the international poverty line of US$1.90 a day.
- Globally, one in nine people in the world today (815 million) are undernourished.
- Poor nutrition causes nearly half (45 per cent) of deaths in children under five – 3.1 million children each year.
- Less than half the people in the world today get all of the health services they need.
- Alarming evidence that important tipping points, leading to irreversible changes in major ecosystems and the planetary climate system, may already have been reached or passed.
- If the global population reaches 9.6 billion by 2050, the equivalent of almost three planets could be required to provide the natural resources needed to sustain current lifestyles.
- Worldwide 218 million children between 5 and 17 years are in employment. 152 million are victims of child labour; almost half of them, 73 million, work in hazardous child labour.
- "It is not 'saving the planet' that will kill growth. Rather the accelerating destruction of nature will undermine not only the global economy, it could eventually threaten many life-forms on earth, including our own species." *Dr Cristiana Pasca-Palmer Executive Secretary of the United Nations Convention on Biological Diversity.*

Our mission is now more urgent than ever. Humans believe they are the crown of creation, top of the food chain; and superior to all other beings. Yet humans rape this world and kill its creatures to the point of unsustainability!

Some experts say, that due to deforestation and global warming, the food of the future will either have to be vegan, or insect based. But why kill and eat others when there is no need? Cannibalism is considered barbaric. Perhaps the same should be considered regarding killing and eating animals?

Women still battle for equality with men, but as humans we must aim even higher, and embrace the sacredness of all life in its totality; to include all beings, and the world itself.

As a provocation on the highest outcome from business for us all, we wish to share with you all a few words about the importance of compassion. How kindness is a strength and not a weakness. And how kindness is also empowering because it is a choice.

But what is kindness? How do we define what is kind? Kindness is caring. Kindness is also harmless. It is compassion. Kindness manifests on three levels - thoughts, words and actions. If we are thinking kind thoughts, those will filter out through our words and ultimately will result in kind actions. This applies to businesses too.

For most of us that is much easier said than done. But it is interesting to consider what would happen if we humans could operate with kindness at all times and if commerce was always compassionate.

For example, let us think of it this way: in business, in a situation where someone is getting aggressive and angry with something that you said, instead of responding emotionally - what if we were all able to be kind and say, "Please forgive me if I have offended you and if I haven't explained myself fully and adequately", before starting the dialogue again?

Another example might be whether we are helping a human being who is in trouble, like an orphaned refugee, or whether we are helping an abandoned puppy - is there any difference? Should there be any difference?

9

Actually, there is no difference, simply because helping either of them is an act of compassion.

Kindness and humility are very close friends. Neither of them are weak. We need to do all the GOOD that we can, so that we may not just survive in business but thrive.

It takes strength of character, mind and tongue to speak and behave kindly and in an edifying fashion – it is a sign of maturity and also a sign that we humans are evolving as a species.

But kindness is a strength, not a weakness. Just because we smile, and are polite, and our business is compassionate does not mean that we won't stand our ground. It pays to be astute.

Being kind to yourself and your business is equally as important as being kind to others. In fact, if you are not kind to yourself it is harder to become kind to others.

Shaolin Monks are committed to a life of harmlessness yet through the practice of Kung Fu, they do not allow anyone to harm them. Defence is not offence.

The challenge is that we must become harmless and at the same time not allow others to be harmful to us, which in turn teaches others to become harmless.

TRIED AND TESTED

Compassionate Colleagues

At Takeout, we are building a compassionate team who will use their blessings to be a blessing to others. A part of our interview process is to ask candidates to, "Tell us about what you do to assist others outside of your family and your job requirements and why."

We have received many inspirational responses to this question ranging from assisting animals, the environment, children and women all over the world. We often find that our clients and partners are inspired by the good works of our team members and thus take on new initiatives to help others as a result.

Since we implemented this and other compassionate policies, employee satisfaction has significantly improved and our business results have rocketed too.

We also aim to ensure that we choose suppliers and partner businesses where possible who have compassionate business practices and who go the extra mile to give back. We examine how harmless their business policies are to animals and the environment, for example do they follow a plant-based diet; we ask about their giving initiatives, and we look into their team diversity.

ACME

Aim to be above judgment, and handle yourself excellently.

We bonus on the following criteria:

- **Excellence** delivering work to a consistently high standard with a 'right first time' approach.
- **Going the extra mile** for clients, colleagues and the community. Punctuality and delivering to deadlines.

- **Positivity** we ask colleagues to role model suggested behaviours from the book "You Can't Afford The Luxury of a Negative Thought" by John Roger and Peter McWilliams.
- **Kindness** we believe that kindness is a strength. We look for kindness and humility in words and actions, towards colleagues, clients and our wider community.

Phrases

"Let's aim for the highest outcome."

"What do you do to help others outside of your work and your family?"

"In addition to your main business model, tell us what does your business do to assist others."

"Please forgive me if I have offended you and if I haven't explained myself fully and adequately."

"Please be assured that we will always do our very best to be champions for you, so don't hesitate to be in touch with any queries, comments and requests."

"Please can you kindly explain why you consider this to be ethical and fair business practice."

"Practice makes perfect!"

Compassion Challenge And Exercise

COMPASSION CHALLENGE: Treat yourself, others and the planet compassionately.

EXERCISE: Meditate on being compassionate.

CHAPTER 2
HUMILITY AND HONOUR

HUMILITY AND HONOUR

Principles

Humankind's noblest pursuit is to be of service. Humility begins with being humble and thinking of others. Giving back is a pre-requisite to success.

To engage in service requires empathy and humility. In business, understanding other points of view fosters better relationships, teamwork and results.

If compassion is central to success then, in our view, humility, honour and hard work follow closely behind.

It's no surprise that researchers have found that, "humility is a distinguishing trait of CEOs of successful organisations." *Psychology Today*

Humility becomes really powerful when it is twinned with honour, a quality considered by Aristotle as one of the greatest. It has its root in three meanings: honesty, prestige, and a source of fulfilment.

As Aristotle knew, honour is one of the key foundations of success, "You will never do anything in the world without courage. It is the greatest quality of the mind, next to honour." *Aristotle*.

Behaving honourably never goes out of fashion. To this day, one of the highest accolades each of us can receive is to be known as a 'person of our word'. It stands to reason if we are to do our best in life and business we must honour our word and promises.

For how many of us is this true? How many of us truly honour our word? For how many businesses is this true? How many have sacrificed honour in order to 'win', at least in the short term, and at what cost?

Take for example famous sporting victories on the world stage that came to pass because of cheating or breaking the rules. The game or medal may have been won in the short-term but once exposed, the cost in the loss of reputation or honour for those involved, lasts a lifetime.

With a commitment to betterment and doing good for the sake of it, courage to tell the truth and do the right thing then comes naturally. This includes honouring oneself and others, especially the vulnerable, including those without a voice.

"For honour travels in a strait so narrow, Where one but goes abreast." *William Shakespeare*

"To forgive takes love. To forget takes humility." *Mother Teresa of Calcutta*

"The best way to find yourself is to lose yourself in the service of others." *Mahatma Gandhi*

TRIED AND TESTED

Seek To Serve

We aim to ensure that our utmost priority is to serve and assist others above and beyond all personal desires, thoughts and ego. This can be in a variety of ways from ensuring that our business practices are happy, helpful and harmless, to leveraging our unique talents and resources to bring about positive action.

In so doing we and many of our colleagues have found an unexpected path to happiness. As Cher's spiritual teacher Ray used to say, "You'll be a lot happier when you stop thinking about yourself all of the time!"

Building small skills - like listening to others before you take your turn to speak and asking others what would suit them best - into everyday practice can transform relationships over time.

Don't be afraid to seek feedback. Constructive criticism may be useful. No one is perfect. Don't be afraid to be ever improving.

Doing The Right Thing

We create structures to keep ourselves accountable to being our word, for example: taking great care to build our values into strategies, policies, and training. We use lists, technology to track progress, slogans on the wall, and feedback to hold us to account, and help us to aim higher.

When we make mistakes big or small, we aim to apologise as swiftly as possible and take thoughtful and immediate action to make amends. We take the view that a true apology comes in the form of changed behaviour.

We seek to ensure that thanks and blessings are given to the sources of our success, this can take the form of thanks in words or in actions, with gifts and celebrations, and we praise God for providing us with abilities, ideas, and opportunities to assist the poor, needy, and vulnerable.

Phrases

"Honour self and others by keeping your word."

"Let me know what would suit you best."

"We perfectly understand your point of view."

"Harvest the humble fruits of honour."

"Kindness and humility are close friends. Neither of them are weak."

Compassion Challenge And Exercise

COMPASSION CHALLENGE: Go the extra mile to help others. Honour your word to yourself and others.

EXERCISE: Visualise yourself humbly forgiving others.

KINDNESS
AND HUMILITY
ARE CLOSE
FRIENDS

CHAPTER 3
PURPOSE AND PROSPERITY

PURPOSE AND PROSPERITY

Principles

Motivation Matters

Looking to the end result of commerce it's always worth us all understanding for what we are aiming to build our ventures. To be rich? To change the world? To secure a future for our family? To fix something that we think is broken in our economy or society? To give all of our money away to help others? At this juncture in our human evolution, we must act now, with a compassionate conscience, to ensure that our planet not only survives, but thrives for future generations.

Through our times meeting and working with the most successful and happy entrepreneurs we've never met one who became an entrepreneur because they wanted to be rich. The ones who used the success for a purpose seemed to be the ones who were most content.

Make no mistake whatever each of us is building will leave an indelible mark, so our responsibility to ourselves as entrepreneurs and business people is to build a good legacy and one that is helpful and harmless.

"It takes 20 years to build a reputation and five minutes to ruin it. If you think about that, you'll do things differently." *Warren Buffett*

Excellent Futures For All

Businesses and individuals can become world influencers due to talents in creativity, technology and sports. If we are to maintain and improve on each of our global standings and create a way ahead, we need to always aim for excellence in each of these sectors. Finding and nurturing the individual skills and talents of young people is a top priority.

Many young people who don't fit the standard academic model are falling through the net. We must stop penalising them for lack of academic progress and adopt new modern models to recognise and enable talent in a broad range of categories.

For example, a dyslexic child that struggles to read might have a photographic memory; just because a child is not strong academically, it doesn't mean that they won't be good at gaming or languages, for example.

We need only look to the lives of globally successful entrepreneurs: Richard Branson who is dyslexic; Oprah Winfrey, a self-described promiscuous teen, victim of sexual abuse and pregnant at the age of 14 who in later life was ranked the richest African-American and the greatest black philanthropist in American history; or Lewis Hamilton the Formula 1 five-times world champion and vegan who took up karate as a young boy to defend himself as a result of bullying at school; to imagine the scale of talent that could be unlocked.

The underlying structure and subject content of the school curriculum has not changed in many countries since the 1970s.

Modern times call for modern measures in education. Schools should be one of the first sectors to keep up with the times. It is time for change. It is time to phase out the old system and time for modern education to help create Excellent Futures for ALL.

We can achieve this by focusing on key Skill-Sets that are needed to become a modern global influencer:

- academic - literature, maths, natural sciences, humanities and social sciences.
- creative - design, music, publishing, architecture, film and video, crafts, visual arts, fashion, TV and radio, advertising, literature, computer games and the performing arts.
- athletic - martial arts, sports and fitness skills, coaching, sports management, and ground maintenance.

- technology - app/product design and development, augmented reality (AR), artificial intelligence (AI), virtual reality (VR), big data, coding, cyber-security, data analytics, gaming, and social media.
- languages - key world languages for modern times: English, Spanish, Mandarin, Arabic, and French.
- life skills - positive communication skills, budgeting, wellbeing and nutrition, relationship skills, meditation, all world religions and faiths, use of social media, and sex education.

For the first years of primary school, teachers should be trained to spot the skills and talents of each child. After this, a student's education should be tailored to their unique strengths. Teachers should be highly skilled in each of the new key Skill-Sets so that they can be role models that children can look up to.

Education Requires Inspiration so there could be regular school trips, days out, and work experience sessions with inspiring companies and individual role models, for example, trips to Apple UK headquarters, meeting with and coaching from professional athletes, and visits to game developers, film sets and more. Video and other content from these inspirational sources would be available online and in virtual reality.

Aspirational Days - Aim high, reach for the stars, and meet them! Highest achievers within each Skill-Set could earn the privilege of 'meeting' their favourite athlete/fashion designer/actor/entrepreneur/game developer etc. via (VR) virtual reality.

Life skills would be a key part of the curriculum for all children. Martial Arts could be compulsory for all girls to help prepare them to defend themselves against potential future violence if necessary, and also to assist in fitness levels and self-confidence.

Daily meditation could take place. Before or after this, there would be a short period of 'Me Time' for every child to do exactly what they would like to (so long as it was harmless to others, was safe and on the school premises). This would help children to recognise what they enjoy doing and are good at.

'Me Time' would also help to change the view of being alone from a punishment to that of a happy and productive time. This is important. Most geniuses who find inventions do so when they are on their own. It is rare that miraculous breakthroughs come in a team. Visionaries from Beethoven to Steve Jobs spent significant time alone. They credited this with helping their inspiration.

Education through inspiration could also include instrumental music throughout the school to uplift and inspire. Lessons could be taught with an element of humour, positivity, and fun. Every school could grow plants: from vegetables such as potatoes, peas and pumpkins; herbs like lavender, peppermint and sage; and flowers.

Children could be asked, "What do you do to help others?" They would become involved in community activities for example: cleaning up plastic on a local beach, volunteering at an animal shelter, or visiting the elderly. These activities would show the importance of helping everyone.

Reprimanding and disciplining is not enough. A further positive step needs to be re-educating. For every correctional piece of advice, a positive next step would also be recommended to each student.

An example of this could be teaching children about the difference between higher and lower (good and bad) emotions and how in most day to day situations it is possible to switch from a negative feeling to a more positive one. For example, if a child was crying or angry about an everyday matter, teachers would be trained to stop them immediately, and kindly encourage them to choose a different emotion to feel or focus on. Each new choice of emotion would be accompanied by a physical action, for example, you could encourage the child to: choose to be happy and smile; choose to be peaceful by taking a deep breath; or be compassionate by extending a hand of friendship.

Optional National Service

Post-school, an Optional National Service scheme could support the continued development of this wide array of Skills-Sets.

The expansion of Skill-Sets for all could address the widening UK skills gap, help eradicate unemployment, help the global economy and promote a new global understanding.

Optional National Service could be a positive opportunity available to every young person. It would also build national skills, and potentially lead to crime reduction e.g. in gangs. Leading public figures including Royals could spearhead involvement.

Benefits for young people would include:

- development and endorsement of character, fitness, work ethic and leadership
- additional skills for life e.g.:
  o technology
  o apprenticeship training
  o driving
  o languages
- travel and adventure - building a global perspective
- credits for accelerated repayment of student loans
- an option for some categories of juvenile and young offenders to complete instead of incarceration

Universal Basic Income (UBI) - Linked To Community Service

Increasing automation, robotics and artificial intelligence, means that in five to ten years many jobs including a great number in transport, storage, manufacturing, retail and admin will be obsolete.

A recent report by PwC estimates almost a third of UK jobs (affecting 10 million workers) could be taken over by automation in the next 15 years with jobs in retail being some of those most at risk.

For this reason, Universal Basic Income merits detailed consideration.

The overarching idea of UBI was first mentioned in Thomas More's book Utopia, published in 1516. Countries recently trialling such a scheme include Finland, Italy, Holland, and Kenya - where adults in one village are being given $22 a month for 12 years. *BBC*

Experts state that UBI may be a route to replacing or delivering efficiencies in the welfare systems. Funding of UBI is proposed to be sourced from the overhaul of each country's tax pool.

UBI could be issued in the following ways:

- be available to all who volunteer for their community
- provide the option for citizens to work and earn on top
- help to reduce homelessness
- option to be provided in the following ways:
    o 33% as food vouchers
    o 33% as utility credits
    o 34% as cash or part cash
    o option for some of the credit to be provided directly to participating landlords
    o any legally required child maintenance would be removed at source

Universal Basic Income has the potential to help eradicate poverty in all its forms, enable people to develop their own unique talents and re-skill for the future economy, support community collaboration and good works, for example: charity workers' salaries could be replaced by UBI ensuring that more of each donation goes directly to the cause it was intended for; and it could unleash creativity in the arts, tech and sports, as well as increase levels of human health and happiness.

It could become the norm. If so, citizens would no longer be scared that they couldn't manage to pay their rent or afford basic living. And it could potentially eradicate homelessness.

With that new mindset, it will be interesting to see the creative ideas, inventions, community initiatives, music and art that citizens never imagined they could create, emerge over the next twenty plus years. Exciting times!

TRIED AND TESTED

Me Time

We take inspiration from creative geniuses and spend time alone in meditation, prayer and contemplation; as well as enjoying nature, inspiring art and music. The power of the ideas that flow through are out of this world!

Ever Evolving

Our capacity for learning is limitless. Knowledge is infinite. Technology has given us the power to learn from the very best; even NASA has provided curriculums for kids.

Everything is available online from how to write a book, to becoming a music producer and DJ. We have endless tools available to us in the forms of books, films, how to guides, and YouTube.

There are countless examples of people who have turned their passion into a business empire. What moves and motivates you can mould your future. Dig deep, be inspired, discover your potential. Explore all the excellent future versions of you. Find your purpose and prosperity will follow!

Phrases

"Let's transform the world for the better, together!"

"Uplift your life with learning."

"Power the planet with purpose."

"Ignite good ideas into profits."

"Cultivate your creativity."

Compassion Challenge And Exercise

COMPASSION CHALLENGE: Learn a new skill to help the world.

EXERCISE: Meditate on prosperity for all!

"In the first International Women's Day debate I attended, I promised to read out the names of the women killed by men since the last International Women's Day. Today I will honour that promise. Over the years, I have had the pleasure of meeting the families of these women, who were grateful that their loved ones were being remembered. I read these names to not only continue to highlight how male violence can terrorise ordinary women's lives, but to pay tribute to these women and those who did not survive and give them the opportunity to be heard. The reason that these women are no longer with us is that they are hard to see, hard to hear and hard to believe. I could not do this without the brilliant work of the Counting Dead Women project and Karen Ingala Smith, who tirelessly records the lives of these women. The first name I will read out is that of a woman who was murdered just days after I rose to my feet here in this Chamber a year ago. These women need us in this place to hear their names and hear their stories, so that we can change and make it so that next year's list might at least be a little bit shorter."

Jess Phillips MP, speaking in the UK House of Commons on International Women's Day 2019. Hansard.

CHAPTER 4
FAITH IN THE FUTURE

FAITH IN THE FUTURE

Principles

In these tumultuous times, we all need a beacon of hope. Faith that we can rise up towards perfection and create a better future for all.

Believe in magic, greatness and excellent visions for the future. Divine inspiration is ready to be accessed for all - as the true wonder of technology, innovation and scientific invention around us show.

Even twenty years ago, who would have imagined the power and wonder that we can access through a smartphone, or the creativity, communication and collective vision that has been possible through the emergence of the World Wide Web.

Our creative visions can be truly powerful. Many of the world's top sports people use detailed visualisation, involving all the senses, as well as meditation techniques, as a route to success. The same techniques can be applied in business too. The more we use our imagination the more results will flow.

For true seers and visionaries, the path to prosperity is not always an easy one. Even geniuses like Leonardo da Vinci had ideas that were rejected and ridiculed, yet eventually, these inventions came to be implemented and ultimately, revered. This is where fearlessness comes in. From time immemorial, the world has needed courageous leaders who will act.

One of the most striking factors of the best visionaries, leaders and entrepreneurs that we know is that they carry on through pain and challenges long after most 'normal' people would have given up.

It is written that in biblical times when the world was facing catastrophe due to man-made errors, it was left to one man, Noah, to have faith in the future; follow a strict path of harmlessness and build the Ark, while all around him - including members of his own family - doubted him. Some of them even considered him to be mad. The scriptures attest that his actions saved the animals, and in so doing he saved mankind too.

In later times, inspirational leaders from Queen Elizabeth I to Mahatma Gandhi and Nelson Mandela all transformed the world due, in a large part, to their faith, vision, resilience and courage.

To survive and thrive we all have to find a way to keep positive, keep our vision and keep on keeping on.

Courage and discipline - close cousins of kindness - are essential.

"Sure I am of this, that you have only to endure to conquer. You have only to persevere to save yourselves, and to save all those who rely upon you. You have only to go right on, and at the end of the road, be it short or long, victory and honour will be found." *Winston Churchill*

You are you forever. The only person who can stop you is YOU!

TRIED AND TESTED

Vision Boards

We aim to inspire ourselves and others by building vision boards. These can be artistic impressions and ideas for the future - for example, paintings, collages, poetry, songs, videos or photos; they could take the form of inspirational quotes or slogans and often they are visual representations of plans, goals and targets. We find that they are very powerful tools in crystallising new futures.

Speak Up!

"Boldly emblazon your creative vision onto the minds of others."

Take Action

The only way to move forward and make the world a better place is to act. Planning, meditating and visioning are all powerful but they deliver little value to the world without the steps of faithful action.

We find that a simple yet powerful way to inspire others into action with you, is to always outline three suggested options for moving ahead. Then pick at least one of them and act!

Seek Feedback

Constructive criticism may be useful. No one is perfect. Don't be afraid to be ever improving.

Phrases

"Fear nothing, You are limitless."

"If you believe it you can achieve it."

41

"Looking forward to forging ahead and transforming the world together."

"The only difference between a Saint and a sinner is that the Saint keeps trying."

"Ever tried. Ever failed. No matter. Try again. Fail again. Fail better."
Samuel Beckett

Compassion Challenge And Exercise

COMPASSION CHALLENGE: Fulfil your dreams so long as they are kind.

EXERCISE: Focus on your infinite possibilities.

CHAPTER 5
GRATITUDE AND GIVING BACK

GRATITUDE AND GIVING BACK

Principles

We are blessed beyond measure to exist in a world of perpetual abundance.

No-one on the planet makes water but everything needs it, we can only use it, recycle it and pray for more of it. We can't create water so the least we can do is be grateful for it, be humble about it and prompt others to be grateful and take care of it too.

It's the same with the air we breathe, the sun, the stars, the moon, the natural world, the plants we eat, the elements and more. All the basics for us to live, for business to run, are provided for free.

That's before we even consider how blessed we are to be standing on the shoulders of giants who came before us on this earth: Prophets, Masters, visionaries, mystics, scholars, artists, composers, musicians, scientists, writers, inventors; all of which raised us up with their good works.

It's astonishing how much we all take this for granted and how it has taken until now when the world faces an environmental crisis for many businesses and much of humanity to start to take action. The Animal Kingdom are playing their part by working in harmony with the planet.

We humans must learn to live in harmony, with each other, with animals, and the planet. We have much to put right. We are blessed so that we may be a blessing.

What if instead of trying to protect ourselves and our businesses with selfishness or engaging in futile attempts to make sure our worldly goods cannot be 'owned' by others. What if we gave more away in thanks for what we have already received for free.

47

What if we all thanked our Divine Creator/The Universe by the giving of our 'First Fruits'.

We hope and pray that good business will sow the seed for all of humanity to do more for the oceans, planet, atmosphere and other beings.

An inspiration is Prophet Muhammad (peace be upon him) who was known for his great generosity.

In current times, business leaders such as Warren Buffett and Bill and Melinda Gates have chosen to give more than half of their wealth away to help others, but you don't need to be a Prophet or a billionaire to assist. In fact, we believe that giving back is a pre-requisite to success rather than success being a prerequisite to giving back.

"There is the expression of selfishness and there is the expression of selflessness - but economists or theoreticians never touched that part. They said, Go and become a philanthropist. I said, No, I can do that in the business world, create a different kind of business - a business based on selflessness." As spoken by Muhammad Yunus to the *New Statesman*

If that's not enough to convince us all, research shows that gratitude can even make us happier and healthier. "One study showed people who wrote down five things they were thankful for once a week were 25% happier after 10 weeks." They were more optimistic about the future, they felt better about their lives and they even did almost 1.5 hours more exercise a week. *PsyBlog Inc.*

"This does my heart and my soul good." *Steven Tyler* said at the opening of his foundation's Janie's House, a home for abused girls in Memphis.

So come on, what are we all waiting for?

TRIED AND TESTED

Tithing

We tithe, which is the spiritual practice of giving back to God the first ten per cent of our income.

Tithing is mentioned many times in scripture including Abram/Abraham tithing to Melchizedek, and Jacob's vow to God that he would give back a tenth of all that God had given him.

It is part of Jewish tradition, and the principle of Zakat (offering 2.5% of an individual's cumulative wealth each year) is one of the five pillars of Islam.

Many celebrities tithe. Companies like IBM have custom payroll systems to make it easy for employees to tithe.

Divine Law states that after a tithe has been made the remaining ninety per cent of income is blessed, and like many others who observe this practice we are in awe of the blessings and miracles that have been granted soon after tithes have been made.

It's such a simple, feel good and effective law to follow that it is somewhat perplexing that it is not yet standard global business practice.

We donate to charities and causes that assist the most vulnerable: children, women, animals, and the environment. We carry out due diligence to do our best to ensure that each cause that we give to is harmless in their activities (e.g. no medical testing on animals) and whose CEOs and executives are paid only reasonable salaries. We consider our tithes as the bare minimum and only the start of what is done to assist others.

"Honour the LORD with thy substance, and with the firstfruits of all thine increase: So shall thy barns be filled with plenty, and thy presses shall burst out with new wine." *Proverbs 3:9-10*

Giving Back

Companies that are significantly contributing to global warming, such as coal, oil, gas, plastic, fast fashion, and waste, need to give an annual percentage of their income to cleaning up the planet.

This 'Planet Protection' percentage from such companies should be discussed in Parliament and at the UN imminently with a plan to making a regulation for all such Corporations.

It should be within yearly running costs of such companies as an expenditure. It should be seen as giving back to the land that has been harmed by their practices. If we looked at this from a personal rather than a business perspective - we wouldn't go into someone's home, take all its resources, trash it and then leave it in a state of devastation. These companies must take responsibility, and give back to repair our earth that they are damaging.

For example:
Energy companies should have at least 5% of their running costs allocated each year towards cleaning up our land, air and oceans from pollution.

Water bottle companies should have at least 5% of their running costs allocated each year towards cleaning up the land and oceans from plastic.

Farmers and slaughterhouse owners as well as animal agriculture chemical companies should have at least 5% of their running costs allocated each year towards cleaning up the soil and polluted water.

Clothing manufacturers and retailers that have exploited their workers and the land, for example in countries such as China, India and Indonesia, as well as others, should have at least 5% of their running costs allocated each year towards cleaning up their rivers and oceans.

This aforementioned giving back that is needed by climate damaging companies is separate from tithing. They will be paying to correct the damage that they are responsible for.

Examples Of Works We Do To Give Back:

The #Handsoff Campaign

CO-CREATED BY CHER CHEVALIER, JUDITH CLEGG &
DANIEL GEEY - LAUNCHED IN THE HOUSE OF COMMONS,
CO-HOSTED BY JESS PHILLIPS MP

The HANDS OFF Campaign features videos, championed by Actors and UNICEF Ambassadors Orlando Bloom and Liz Solari, as well as famous sports people, celebrities, Lords, Baronesses, business leaders, social campaigners and members of the general public, all speaking out to end violence against adults and children.

Alarming numbers of animals, children and adults are abused every day. The #HANDSOFF Campaign has three goals:

1. Abusers will stop
2. Victims will speak up
3. Violence becomes unacceptable

- Over two women are killed every week in the UK by a current or former partner. *Refuge*
- Nearly half a million children in the UK are estimated to be suffering abuse. *NSPCC*
- 1 in 5 women in the UK have experienced some form of sexual violence since the age of 16. *Rape Crisis*
- 85,000 women and 12,000 men are raped in England and Wales every year. That's roughly 11 rapes (of adults alone) every hour. *Rape Crisis*
- Over 47,000 sexual offences were recorded against children in the UK between 2014 and 2015. *NSPCC*
- Nearly 120,000 prosecutions relating to violent crime against women were reported in the UK from 2015 - 2016. *The Guardian*
- Between 2010 and 2015, the number of recorded sexual offences against children in England has increased by 85%. *NSPCC*

- On average police in England and Wales receive over 100 calls relating to domestic abuse every hour. *Justice Inspectorates (HMIC)*
- Over 100,000 prosecutions for domestic abuse-related offences were made in the year ending March 2016. *CPS*
- During the 2010 World Cup, cases of domestic violence rose by an average of 25% after an England match, win or lose. *The Independent*
- Over 560 victims have been identified in historic cases of child sex abuse within UK football. *BBC*
- According to UNICEF, every five minutes, a child dies as a result of violence. *UN, UNICEF*
- Approximately one in 10 girls under the age of 20, or 120 million girls worldwide, have been subjected to sexual violence. *UN*
- Globally half of all female homicide victims were killed by their partner or family member. *UN*
- A UN report estimates that one in three women worldwide has experienced physical or sexual violence in their lifetime. *UN Women, UN*
- It is estimated that 4.5 million people worldwide are trapped in forced sexual exploitation. *Polaris Project*

The Campaign was Co-Created by Cher Chevalier, Judith Clegg, and Daniel Geey - Partner in the Sports Group at law firm Sheridans, Author, and Chairman of Football Aid. All three have been directly affected by violence themselves or have had close friends and family who have suffered violent abuse.

Numerous Takeout team members volunteer to assist the campaign which features videos from people from all walks of life.

The #HANDSOFF Campaign aims to make violence uncool.

Get Involved:

Join us and celebrities including actors and UNICEF Ambassadors Liz Solari and Orlando Bloom, film director Kip Andersen, footballers Ezequiel Lavezzi (Hebei China Fortune and Argentina), Danny Rose (Tottenham Hotspur and England), Hector Bellerin (Arsenal and Spain), Jordan Nobbs and Leah Williamson (Arsenal and England) Chris Ramsey (QPR), tennis player Diego Schwartzman, DJ Judge Jules, technologist and Professor Sue Black OBE and many more…

Follow @handsoffcampaign on Instagram
Follow @handsoffglobal on Twitter and Facebook
Record your HANDS OFF video and share
on social media www.handsoffcampaign.com
#HANDSOFF

Paws - Policy For Animal Welfare Scheme

CO-CREATED BY CHER CHEVALIER & JUDITH CLEGG - LAUNCHED IN THE HOUSE OF COMMONS, CO-HOSTED BY HENRY SMITH MP

Vegetarian Henry Smith MP and Co-creators of PAWS, Cher Chevalier and Judith Clegg presented the Policy for Animal Welfare Scheme to key politicians and animal welfare charities/campaigners including Marc Abraham of Pup Aid and Lucy's Law, The Mayhew, Viva!, Raystede, All Dogs Matter, Four Paws, Animal Equality, Humanimal Trust, five-time Paralympic Gold Medallist Natasha Baker MBE, Cllr Jane Smith - Animal Welfare Party, Rosie Cooper MP, Jim Shannon MP and Nigel Huddleston MP to name but a few.

We created the PAWS policy document in 2016 and it was swiftly delivered to UK Government and 10 Downing Street. PAWS highlights the fact that the British are a nation of pet lovers, yet there are significant pet welfare problems. Some are due to enforcement issues of laws already in place. Some are due to legal gaps where expansion of the law is needed.

Pet Breeding Problems:

- **Puppy Farming** - up to 400,000 farmed puppies are sold to the British public every year. *Nature-watch*
- **Unplanned Kittens** - an estimated 4.3 million unplanned kittens are born to UK households. One unspayed female cat could be responsible for 20,000 descendants in just five years. *PDSA, The National Animal Trust*
- **Illegal Pet Trade** - the EU's most profitable illegally traded commodities are drugs, arms and puppies. *Newsweek*
- **Abandoned Pets** - a Dogs Trust survey shows in the last year 47,596 dogs were heartlessly left unclaimed by their owners in

council pounds. Cats Protection estimates that there are 9 million stray and 1.5 million feral cats in the UK.

- **Healthy Pets Euthanised** - 98% of vets are asked to euthanise healthy pets. *British Veterinary Association*
- **Dog Fighting** - the League against Cruel Sports estimate that there are hundreds of organised dog fighters in the UK.
- **Animal Cruelty** - RSPCA inspectors investigate more than 149,000 complaints of cruelty and neglect every year.
- **Tax Evasion** - criminal gangs make up to £35k a week by selling dozens of fashionable breeds. *RSPCA*

Paws Policy Points:

- Creation of an Independent Animal Inspectorate to deploy Animal Officers in partnership with Animal Welfare Charities.
- National Pet Register to include a tracking system for pet welfare.
- Minister for Animals for the UK's 51 million pets.
- Ring-fenced Tax Revenue - initial revenue estimate of over £350 million per year.
- A National Abusers List to help predict and prevent further abuse and trafficking of animals as well as of children and adults.
- Animal Crime Stoppers.
- Lost Pet Database.
- PAWS will pay for itself.

PAWS - Policy for Animal Welfare Scheme is a win-win for pets, responsible owners, breeders, government, taxpayers, and charities. PAWS LAW is also making headway on assisting other animals, not just companion animals, in multiple countries.

Get Involved:

To support PAWS LAW
Follow @pawslawuk on Instagram, Twitter and Facebook
#PAWSLAW and write to your local MP or Politician
asking them to support the policy.
#PAWSLAW

PAWS LAW is needed worldwide.

For full PAWS - Policy for Animal Welfare Scheme details and the
official launch video visit:
http://www.handsoffcampaign.com/paws.html

'LOST CHILD' SONG

Join 1 million voices to end violence against children

'LOST CHILD' is an inspired song written by Cher Chevalier and collaborated on with platinum selling songwriter Dani Senior, and Grammy award winning producer Richard Adlam to raise awareness about the crisis faced by vulnerable children around the world that suffer violence in the forms of: Child Trafficking, Child Marriage, Rape, FGM, Child Labour, Child Prostitution, and War.

This 'LOST CHILD' song calls for an end to all sexual, physical, and emotional abuse experienced by children.

The 'LOST CHILD' song declares war on violence against children.

- During the last decade, child victims of war included: 2 million killed; 4-5 million disabled; 12 million left homeless; over 1 million orphaned. *UNICEF*
- Approximately 350 million children are living in war zones from South Sudan and the Republic of Congo to Syria and Myanmar. *Save The Children*
- In 2015, 91% of children who arrived in Europe on their own were boys. *Missing Children Europe*
- WHERE ARE ALL THE MISSING GIRLS?
- 10,000 children went missing in Europe between 2014 and 2016. *Europol*
- 1 child every 2 minutes is reported missing in the EU. *Missing Children Europe*
- 4.4 million children are in need of humanitarian assistance in the Democratic Republic of Congo. *War Child*
- 5.3 million children are in need of humanitarian assistance in Afghanistan. *War Child*

- 2 million children are subjected to prostitution in the global commercial sex trade. *UNICEF*
- The average trafficking victim is aged 11 to 14. The average life span of a trafficking victim is 7 years. *Ark of Hope for Children*
- 152 million children aged between 5 and 17 are subjected to child labour. *UN*
- Approximately 50% of Rohingya girls raped while fleeing Myanmar were under 18, including one girl who was just 9 years old, and many others under the age of 10. *MSF*
- 15 million girls are forced to marry each year - that's 28 girls every minute. *Action Aid*

Join 1 million voices to end violence against children
Follow @lostchildsong
Post videos on social media channels shouting:
"LOST CHILD, WHERE ARE YOU NOW?"
#lostchildsong
http://www.handsoffcampaign.com/lost-child.html

Phrases

"Let your light shine before men that they may see your good works."
Matthew 5:16

"Looking forward to ending violence/cruelty together!"

"Spend some, save some, give some. Create an upward spiral."

"Give to grow!"

"Have a gratitude attitude."

Meditate On Gratitude

Be grateful for your life.

Realise that you are breathing the same air as all other beings. Recognise that we all have the same needs.

We all need air, water, food and to have shelter.

Feel your gratitude grow as you notice our needs make us one. Focus on all beings having their needs met.

Be grateful for the earth that is our mutual home. Be grateful as you journey through this world.

We are all travelling in this world together - let us assist each other along the way.

Compassion Challenge And Exercise

COMPASSION CHALLENGE: On a weekly basis challenge yourself to move out of your comfort zone and uplift others, for example:

1. If you are usually kind to the environment, challenge yourself to be kind to animals as well.
2. If you are charitable to children's causes, challenge yourself to be charitable towards the elderly.
3. Pray or meditate on being more compassionate to yourself and your family.

EXERCISE: Write a gratitude list. Include everything and everyone that you are grateful for.

Taken from Cher Chevalier's Book: SLIM - Step Lightly in Mind, Body, Spirit.

"Those who conduct themselves with morality, integrity and consistency need not fear the forces of inhumanity and cruelty."
Nelson Mandela
By Himself: The Authorised Book of Quotations

DO GOOD
BE GOOD
FEEL GOOD

CHAPTER 6
DEDICATED DIVERSITY

DEDICATED DIVERSITY

Principles

Our magnificent planet is home to over 8.7 million species including animals (human and non-human), fungi, plants, protozoa and chromists. Imagine how many more there may be in our universe and beyond.

The earth is in Divine Perfection when these diverse species, each with their own vital talent, work in harmony with each other and with the elements. The wind, bats, birds, bees, and other insects help to pollinate flowers and are essential for the growth of many fruits and vegetables; species such as the sea anemones and clownfish live in symbiosis and, of course, plants produce the oxygen needed for many species, including humans, to breathe.

Just as diversity underpins the circle of life so too it drives the wheel of business. Companies with more diverse teams including gender, racial and ethnic diversity are significantly more successful, profitable and we would argue more fun to be a customer or employee of too!

Whilst the principles of diversity and equality have come to the fore in modern times, they are rooted deep in history.

Mary Magdalene was the Apostle to the Apostles - Yeshua's/Jesus' Chief Apostle, along with John. It is written that she was present at the crucifixion and at the resurrection. The fact that she was never a prostitute - Mary Magdalene's name was blasphemously slandered by Pope Gregory in the sixth century when he decided to accuse her of prostitution, even though this is NOT written in the Gospels - has finally been cleared up, fifteen centuries later; thanks to the current Pope Francis:

"So that woman, who is the first to encounter Jesus...now has become an apostle of the new and greatest hope." *Pope Francis, Catholic News Agency*

The Egyptians, one of the most advanced civilisations in the ancient world, were often led by co-ruling Pharaohs and Queens, for example, Queen Nefertiti and her husband, Pharaoh Akhenaten ruled together, side by side in the mid-1300s BC.

In the 15th Century, Guru Nanak, the vegetarian founder of Sikhism stood for peace, harmony and equality of all people. He emphasised the importance of helping others, denounced the unfair and inhumane treatment of animals and spoke out against inequality for all including women saying that it "is a woman who keeps the race going" and "from woman are born leaders and kings."

Many of England's most successful, as well as longest reigning monarchs have been women: Queen Elizabeth I, Queen Victoria and Queen Elizabeth II.

The staff at Bletchley Park, the UK centre for World War Two Code-breakers, some would say, were made up of an eccentric list of skill-sets and experiences. They included crossword puzzlers, chess players, linguists, classicists, papyrologists and mathematicians. By the end of the war in 1945, 75% of the team were women. Between them, they are said to have shortened the war by two to four years potentially saving up to 21 million lives.

Despite the overwhelming benefits of diversity to business and all of society we still have a long way to go.

- Whilst only a small number of species have been assessed, the International Union for Conservation of Nature (IUCN) already lists 97,000 species on its threatened Red List. Shockingly more than 25,000 are threatened with extinction including 40% of amphibians, 34% of conifers, 33% of reef-building corals, 25% of mammals and 14% of birds.
- UNICEF estimates that 168 million children aged 5 to 17 are engaged in child labour worldwide and that every five minutes, a child dies as a result of violence.

- The UN reports that more than one in three women worldwide has experienced physical or sexual violence in their lifetime. Some national studies show that up to 70 per cent of women have experienced physical and/or sexual violence from an intimate partner in their lifetime.
- According to the World Economic Forum gender inequality at the workplace and in political representation means that the current global gender gap will take more than 100 years to close at the current pace of change.
- In the UK in 2018 there were as many FTSE 100 CEOs called Dave/David as women, and the UK is one of the most advanced countries, coming 15th out of 149 in the World Economic Forum's 2018 Gender Gap report.
- According to the UN, if women farmers had the same access to resources as men, the number of hungry people in the world could be reduced by up to 150 million.

In today's Britain and in many other so-called progressive countries there is still bullying and a bias against women inherent in family relationships and in several other aspects of life too.

Further afield, respected award winning author and academic Elif Shafak went as far as saying in an interview with the BBC, "in terms of women's rights we have been sliding backwards", "the streets belong to men," and that "we need diversity for democracy". Yet we are facing a time in history where, as the Spectator Magazine says, "But when women's rights conflict with the goal of accommodating other cultures, it's almost always women who are pushed to the side".

We must tackle inequality and patriarchy at its root; with legislation.

A further opportunity is the extraterritorial effect of our laws and our ability to influence others to do a better job on gender equality too.

As recently as this century men have legally been able to have multiple wives in 58 nations. Women are permitted more than one husband in only a handful of nations.

If we have patriarchs, we must have matriarchs. If we permit polygyny, then we must permit polyandry too. It's little known that England recognises a polygamous marriage if it occurred abroad and it is a valid marriage where it occurred.

We should all be seeking the very best in women's rights and legislation. This should include stronger laws to protect women and children from harm, including free Martial Arts training in refuges for women who are fleeing from domestic violence.

This Martial Arts training could dramatically reduce violence. A Canadian study of college students published in The New England Journal of Medicine found, for example, that being taught verbal and physical self-defence almost halved the risk of rape from 9.8% to 5.2%. The risk of attempted rapes fell even further from 9.3% to 3.4%.

In the UK, this could also serve as a fitting legacy for Queen Elizabeth II and be delivered in her lifetime.

The legislation could also be supported by further prominent female public sector appointments and role models. For example, in military leadership, or in the continued MI6 campaign to recruit more women.

In modern nations, women should be leading the way.

The fact that the UK and Western countries are some of the best in the world in terms of rights for women, should not make them complacent. There is still much to be done to address violence against women, equal pay, parental rights, female representation on boards, in many key professions and much, much more.

Business has a fundamental role to play in championing diversity for the betterment of all, not least to atone for the detrimental impact it has already had on diversity.

"So it will come to pass that when women participate fully and equally in the affairs of the world, when they enter confidently and capably the great arena of laws and politics, war will cease…". *Abdu'l-Bahá*

TRIED AND TESTED

Diverse Inspiration

Takeout was founded on the principle of diversity. Our team comes from a broad mix of skill-sets, disciplines, nationalities and backgrounds. We believe this is essential to inspire, inform and deliver innovation and business success.

We are well known for the power of our network and have a wealth of mystics, brainiacs, innovators, entrepreneurs, academics, investors, musicians, sports people, entertainment stars and visionaries of all kinds who we involve in creating excellent results for our clients.

Colleagues in London, New York, Shanghai, LA, Berlin and many more cities collaborate with each other to crack innovation challenges. Learning from each other and sharing skills and experiences raises each of us up personally and professionally.

We love it.

Raising Up Others

We seek to offer roles and opportunities to individuals who come from a range of backgrounds including those who have been disadvantaged. Many of these team members go on to out-perform colleagues with more traditional business qualifications and experiences.

By doing this we are not only being kind but tapping into a unique and loyal talent pool that many others miss out on. More importantly, they tell us that working with us has changed their lives and those of their families for the better too.

Phrases

"Upscale Female!"

"Connected and Respected."

"Magnify our manifold talents."

"Celebrate our Divine differences."

Compassion Challenge And Exercise

Your good works can change the world. Won't it be amazing for example, when teenage girls are the new world leaders in championing biodiversity by creating ethical inventions to replace single-use plastics?

It is said that there is a time and place for everything under heaven. Is this your time to change the world using the power and inspiration of diversity?!

COMPASSION CHALLENGE: Go the extra mile at all times to assist diversity on our planet, in society and in business. Note the miraculous results that flow.

EXERCISE: Focus on the many ways in which you could support diversity and equality in business. Pick three to implement immediately. How many new good works - products, services or innovations - will these actions bring to life?

"Forgiveness is a virtue of the brave."
Indira Gandhi

CHAPTER 7
COMPASSIONATE
COMMUNICATION

COMPASSIONATE COMMUNICATION

Principles

In any given moment, we have a choice as to whether we are creating light or darkness with our thoughts, words and actions. This includes the way we speak to others and ourselves!

Commerce should be looked upon as a responsibility. Companies are one hundred per cent responsible for what they are selling and communicating to the world, ideally needing to be for the betterment of all. The powerful choice is to choose to be good, positive and helpful at all times where possible.

With that in mind, it can be a very revealing experience for many of us to look back and review the results of our past communications.

Let's look at these facts:

- Psychologist John Gottman says that "for happy relationships we should actually aim for five positive interactions with our partner for every negative one." *Action for Happiness*
- Seven in 10 young people have experienced cyberbullying, with 37% of young people saying they experience cyberbullying regularly. *Sky News*
- An Amnesty International study of 778 female journalists and politicians found that they were sent an abusive/problematic tweet every 30 seconds on average and black women were 84% more likely than white women to receive abusive/problematic tweets. *Time*
- "70 per cent of mentored businesses survive more than five years, double the rate for non-mentored small businesses over that same period." *Inc.*
- Suicide is now the leading cause of death for young people under 20. Levels of self-harm are rising among teenage girls in particular. *Matt Hancock MP, The Guardian*

- In a recent survey by the Cyber Civil Rights Initiative 23% of respondents had been victims of revenge porn and of these, 93% reported significant emotional distress, while 82% reported suffering significant impairment in social, occupational, or other important areas of functioning. Over half of the victims indicated that they had even considered committing suicide. *cyberbullying.org*

Violence, be it verbal or physical, is the lowest form of communication.

With practice, patience and self-discipline we can all learn to make a positive difference and increase the level of compassion in our communications.

As the famous phrase coined by Edward Bulwer-Lytton goes, "The pen is mightier than the sword".

Communication can be an ultimate tool to inspire individuals, nations, and at times the whole world.

The arc of hope generated by a great speech can shine on for years, decades and even centuries: "I have a dream that one day this nation will rise up, live out the true meaning of its creed: We hold these truths to be self-evident: that all men are created equal." *Martin Luther King*

The most memorable of these words paint an uplifting vision for the future and a way to conquer all challenges. They inspire us to look upward, forge ahead and prevail in the right course of action.

There are even times when someone's whole life can be changed for the better by a few well chosen and compassionate words.

Many of us have the opportunity to do just that for others. Will we all be ready to seize the moment and make that vital difference?

Good words, images, music, even body language and our clothes can be used to communicate a message. Humour can also be a powerful technique - stand up comedians have even been known to help change the course of history. Sometimes even your very presence for example at an important event or in someone's hour of need is all that is needed.

With this power on the tips of our tongues, and at the touch of our keypads, it pays to make wise choices. Let's aim to deliver the most compassionate communication possible at any given time. For example, choosing to always leave a conversation or communication on an upbeat note; with a positive vision for the future, a helpful suggestion, a kind action to take, or a word of encouragement.

We must also consider global communications. Freedom of speech is critical to democracy. Freedom of the press must remain but it must be fit for a modern world. A major reform of press including social media is needed, particularly to address abuse and untrue online communications. For example, social media companies should be more closely regulated to combat fake news and bullying. Copyright law must be reviewed so that individuals have control of their own rights and privacy.

We currently have, to some degree, a press system that for many affords little privacy. The publishing of photos and videos taken on private property without that individual's permission, has become a new normal.

Everyone should own their copyright including images of themselves - and with this legislation - profit-driven attacks on personal privacy would become illegal.

In the eyes of the law, a person is innocent until proven guilty. Some press have been known to benefit from incorrectly exposing people by using words such as 'allegedly', at times causing great distress.

Thankfully there are many burgeoning positive news outlets seeking to share constructive and uplifting stories, as well as the all-important facts on world events and challenges. We should support and celebrate this type of positive press.

It is time to turn the tide and champion compassionate communication. It will enrich life. It will save lives.

Words have power. May we all choose them wisely.

TRIED AND TESTED

Communication Techniques

1. Speak only if it is true, necessary and kind.
2. Silence can be incredibly powerful. So speak only if your words are more powerful than your silence.
3. When someone is being angry, unkind or unreasonable, try and see their perspective, remain calm, kind, and above reproach. Be understanding and patient. Offer to assist. Ask for forgiveness or apologise if necessary.

Phrases

"Death and life are in the power of the tongue." *Proverbs 18:21*

"My words are edifying and uplifting."

"Let's assist one another in forging ahead."

"Change our world with compassionate words."

"Please forgive me."

"I wish you well in all things."

Compassion Challenge And Exercise

COMPASSION CHALLENGE: Write a two-sided forgiveness list:

Side 1 - Everyone and everything that you need to forgive.
Side 2 - Everything that you may need to ask God/your Divine Creator to forgive you for.

EXERCISE: Use your mind to calm your emotions and master your speech.

"Thought is just not something objective in our heads. Thought is power – real, objective power. Moreover, the thoughts we create have a life of their own. They have a kind of material reality that affects other people for good or ill – hence our responsibility to choose."

Annie Besant

CHAPTER 8
PLAYING FAIR

PLAYING FAIR

Principles

Imagine how wonderful the world would be if we were all Happy, Helpful and Harmless. We would eradicate cruelty, abuse and neglect. If we were happy we wouldn't be cruel. If we were helpful we wouldn't neglect. If we were harmless we wouldn't abuse.

Imagine if you didn't ever have to worry about being ripped off, or being sold a product that hurt you or others, or if everyone around you at work was always happy and ready to help everyone else.

Those of us in business are blessed by opportunities to provide a path to peace and prosperity for ALL through commerce.

Scientific discoveries and business innovation can and should be used to do good.

Both of our grandfathers, for example, worked in science and business and helped bring to life innovations that assisted in bringing an end to World War II.

Today, companies are harnessing science and innovation to create multiple helpful and harmless products including plant-based meat substitutes which create a win-win for animals, customers, the planet and shareholders alike.

As well as being kind to the planet and a healthy alternative to meat, customers say the meat substitute products are delicious, so much so, they are fast becoming highly fashionable, sometimes even outselling meat burgers in mainstream stores. The plant-based meats market is predicted by some to be worth $35 billion USD and that's just in the United States.

According to GlobalData, the number of vegans in America rose by 600% between 2014 and 2017. The South China Morning Post reports that China a country known for its heavy reliance on meat-based diets is on track to be the fastest growing vegan market on the planet.

A recent UK market research study found that "a startling 75% of the public indicated that they currently modify their consumption and have become more conscious about their use of consumer items including plastic, non-recyclable materials, dairy, meat, sugar, salt, gluten, palm oil, travel, clothes and products that have been tested on animals." *Walnut*

Compassion in Commerce is rising up rapidly. It can be highly profitable too.

The concept of karma is familiar to many of us. It is a central teaching of some eastern religions including Buddhism and Hinduism and is described by many as a natural force, like gravity. Interestingly the meaning of the word is rooted in action, which makes perfect sense since karma is based on cause and effect, or put simply, 'what goes around comes around.'

We believe it strongly applies in business too. We have witnessed many examples of companies and people achieving great success and happiness as a result of their compassionate actions.

"All that we are is the result of what we have thought. If a man speaks or acts with an evil thought, pain follows him. If a man speaks or acts with a pure thought, happiness follows him, like a shadow that never leaves him." *Siddhartha Gautama, The Buddha*

"Perform work that will give benefit of all (divine sacrifice), otherwise work causes bondage in this material world. There, O son of Kunti, perform your prescribed duties for the happiness of all, and in that way you will always remain free from bondage." *Krishna, Bhagavad-Gita (3.9)*

If we are truly to be Compassionate in Commerce we must also stop rip-off business. Time and time again the business community has been responsible for 'brainwashing' the public with appalling consequences. All in the pursuit of profit.

The motive is the root. For example, a chocolate company could be aiming to make people happy and smile, but it is only truly doing this in the long term if the chocolate is also healthy to eat, and is sourced and distributed ethically.

Let's take, for example, the opaque practices involved in marketing meat, dairy, sugar and smoking by, at times, hiding the truth.

To quote expert Jill Pell at the Institute of Health and Wellbeing at Glasgow University: "It would be misleading" for health authorities to set any safe dose for processed meat, "other than zero." *The Guardian*

What's more, as the Guardian explains, "The part of the story we haven't been told – including by the WHO – is that there were always other ways to manufacture these products that would make them significantly less carcinogenic. The fact that this is so little known is tribute to the power of the meat industry which has for the past 40 years, been engaged in a campaign of cover-ups and misdirection to rival the dirty tricks of Big Tobacco."

Then there is the marketing of 'humane' treatment of animals and of the industry as 'sustainable' by meat executives.

Many believe these claims are abhorrent and wrong, and that sentient beings should not be kept in often vile conditions, before they are killed so that people can eat them.

Multiple scientific studies claim that the best way to save the planet is to eliminate meat and dairy from our diets.

Leading experts boldly call out the shocking absurdity of it all:

"What will future generations looking back on our age, see as its monstrosities? One of them, I believe, will be the mass incarceration of animals, to enable us to eat their flesh or eggs or drink their milk. While we call ourselves animal lovers, and lavish kindness on our dogs and cats, we inflict brutal deprivations on billions of animals that are just as capable of suffering. The hypocrisy is so rank that future generations will marvel at how we could have failed to see it." *George Monbiot, Winner of a United Nations Global 500 Roll of Honour Award for outstanding environmental achievement. The Guardian* He also states in the Guardian "The livestock industry will resist all this, using the bucolic images and pastoral fantasies that have beguiled us for so long."

"It used to be that vegans were considered to be sort of on the fringe, you know? But I want to point out to you that when Esselstyn and Ornish reversed coronary artery disease, they reversed it! Coronary artery disease kills 1/3 of people in the United States. They did it on a vegan, low-fat diet." This is what Esselstyn says: "My message is clear and absolute: coronary artery disease need not exist, and if it does, it need not progress." *Ellsworth Wareham - American vegan heart surgeon who lived to be 104.*

"A vegetarian diet can be the single most effective way to prevent chronic disease. An estimated 70% of all diseases including one-third of all cancers are related to diet. A plant-based diet reduces the risk of chronic degenerative diseases including coronary heart disease, diabetes, obesity, high blood pressure and cancers such as prostate, breast, colon stomach, lung and esophageal cancer." *Ornish Living*

"If everyone ate a Western diet, we would need two Planet Earths to feed them. We only have one. And she is dying. Poor countries sell their grain to the West for hard currency while their own children starve in their arms. And the West feeds it to livestock... So we can eat a steak? I bet I am not the only one in the room who sees this as a crime?" *Philip*

Wollen, Australian philanthropist, Former Vice-President Citibank, and General Manager at Citicorp.

Some experts say that meat tax is a way forward. As well as the environmental benefits it "would save many lives and raise billions to pay for healthcare". *NHS, The Guardian*

The British National Health Service reports that researchers believe that price increases of about 13% for red meat and 79% for processed meat would result in 22% fewer deaths and a reduction in healthcare costs of 19% linked to processed meat consumption.

Yet some meat and farming executives argue on.

Sugar consumption has a severe impact on human health too. Multiple studies have linked it with diabetes, obesity, heart disease, dental cavities and arthritis. The New Statesman reports that "problems with blood sugar kill nearly four million people a year", and the US Centers for Disease Control and Prevention predicts that one in three Americans could have diabetes by 2050.

Some of these links have been known for over a century and yet leading industry bodies were, according to Stanton Glantz, Professor of Medicine, U.C.S.F. "They were able to derail the discussion about sugar for decades." *The New York Times*

In yet another egregious example and in the words of U.S. District Judge Gladys Kessler, the tobacco industry "marketed and sold their lethal product with zeal, with deception, with a single minded focus on their financial success, and without regard for the human tragedy or social costs that success exacted." *NBC*

In current times The World Health Organisation reveals that "tobacco kills more than 7 million people each year. Around 80% of the world's 1.1 billion smokers live in low and middle-income countries." In the

United States alone tobacco use costs $170 billion in direct medical costs and $156 billion in lost productivity per year. *NBC*

And that's not all. Business actively blocks useful products that could provide great benefits for the world:

How many healing compounds (including research on the medicinal benefits of herbs) that could benefit millions are being held back by the pharmaceutical industry?

How many billions of technology products stop working before their true end of life because of built-in obsolescence?

How greatly are the beneficial impacts of diet and exercise eclipsed by the marketing of expensive drugs and health treatments?

There are frightening examples that business is not fighting fair:

How many billions of pounds are spent on marketing campaigns that encourage consumers to spend on products they neither need nor can afford?

How much does business spend in celebrating and promoting evil and greed?

How many businesses are playing fair with the environment?

How many international tax laws allow large multi-nationals to have a far lower tax burden than small and medium-sized enterprises?

It is time for change. We pray that as the general public become fully informed on the cruelty involved and the true impact on the planet and human health, new compassionate ways of doing business will replace the barbaric ones.

"The greatness of a nation and its moral progress can be judged by the way its animals are treated." *Mahatma Gandhi*

"As long as man continues to be the ruthless destroyer of lower living beings he will never know health or peace. For as long as men massacre animals, they will kill each other." *Pythagoras*

"If slaughterhouses had glass walls, everyone would be a vegetarian." *Sir Paul & Linda McCartney*

TRIED AND TESTED

Kind Food

We aim to be kind to all beings and the planet. All food that Takeout pays for when entertaining or covering our team for subsistence is strictly vegetarian. WeWork the global network of workspaces, one of the most successful US startups with a current valuation of approximately $20 billion, has recently implemented a meat-free policy too.

A wealth of clients and colleagues have thanked us for how healthy, energetic and uplifted they feel when eating kind food!

Win-Win

We aim to promote WIN-WIN solutions. The Buddha called this the Third Way or Middle Way. We seek to assist WIN-WINS for the planet, animals and people in all that we do. For example, the PAWS - Policy for Animal for Welfare Scheme which we Co-created is a WIN-WIN for pets, responsible owners, governments, taxpayers and animal welfare charities.

Phrases

"Operate to cooperate."

"Let's find a win-win solution."

"Fight the GOOD fight."

"Say unto them, As I live, saith the Lord GOD, I have no pleasure in the death of the wicked; but that the wicked turn from his way and live." *Ezekiel 33:11*

Compassion Challenge & Exercise

COMPASSION CHALLENGE

1. Devise three ways in which you and your business can be a Blessing. Create a plan and a deadline to make them happen. Then share your plan with others to create accountability to keep your word!
2. Consider a current business challenge and commit to finding a WIN-WIN solution for ALL. Set this as your template for the future.
3. Focus on uplifting others. Make notes.

EXERCISE: GO PLANT-BASED

"We've got a long way to go but things are changing. I don't want to sound complacent but we've made a really good start in cutting out meat as a society and I'm sure that in future generations, humanity won't eat meat. We'll look back at this period, when we did eat meat, and be absolutely appalled! We are moving in the right direction but that is only thanks to organisations like Viva! and PAWS and many others - it is you who really make sure that this agenda is in the public's consciousness."

Vegetarian, Henry Smith MP, speaking to Viva!Life Magazine at the launch of PAWS - Policy for Animal Welfare Scheme in the House of Commons, December 2018

CHAPTER 9
MODERN MODELS

MODERN MODELS

Principles

With the march of robotics, AI and other automation, fundamental change is afoot. As well as the high numbers of jobs at risk, the work that remains will require new skills. The World Economic Forum (WEF) forecast that imminently "no less than 54% of all employees will require significant re-and up-skilling."

New modern models will be essential.

New technology skills will, of course be required, but there will also be a great demand for creative and emotional skills, which will help individuals, companies and countries become world shapers.

Here we reveal some of our predictions and strategies for success:

The Future Of Creativity

The fourth industrial revolution will pave the way for a twenty-first-century renaissance and reformation unlocking invention and ingenuity. Creative industries, sport and science will flourish. Hitherto unseen links between innovation and spirituality will be understood.

The future of creative industries is thus of critical importance. They must be nurtured as a priority. Therein the potential for the advancement of human consciousness, inspiration, hope, compassion and progress for the whole planet lies.

The Future Of Fashion

The future of fashion will be heavily based on Artificial Intelligence (AI), Augmented Reality (AR), and Virtual Reality (VR). The future is NOW.

For example, within 5 years consumers could be able to:

- virtually visit emporium stores which cluster similar categories of stores within stores. For example, high street fashion stores, all under one 'roof'
- virtually enter stores through fabulous and magical entrances and enjoy fully immersive beautifully visually designed experiences
- go global virtual shopping and visit some of the world's best stores like Selfridges in London, and Barney's in New York
- watch the runway shows of New York, London, Paris and Milan in real-time, in virtual reality
- shop in their own personalised image and even be able to create an avatar of their pets to go virtual shopping with them
- 'meet' friends and virtually shop together
- pay to virtually hang out and chat with their favourite stars and experts e.g. fashion designers, sports stars, movie stars and more, all in virtual reality.

Even Queen Elizabeth II could secure her legacy as one of the greatest and most forward-thinking British Monarchs of all time by meeting people in virtual reality. This could link to charitable causes and campaigns that benefit the nation. Imagine a future in which there could even be virtual reality screens in front of Buckingham Palace!

Flagship real stores will still exist in key cities but the majority of retail shops could be gone within a decade. Shoe shops could last the longest because shoes need to be tried on for exact fitting.

High streets will mainly consist of food outlets and services such as hairdressers, spas and wellness centres. Innovation in the service industry will abound too, for example, new technology will mean that hairdressers and spas will be able to provide customers with a fabulous hairdo or manicure in ten minutes.

With up to 19% of UK individual travel trips being for shopping and personal business, the drop in retail stores will also have a significant positive impact on congestion and pollution.

These changes on the high street will mean that many B1 (business) and D1 (non-residential institutions) properties will be switched back into living quarters. This will help the UK economy from a housing perspective. For example, in ten years' time, Oxford Street in London wouldn't be lined with shops, it could be filled with cool, high-spec eco apartments.

Retailers could share costs in the development of technology and virtual reality shopping platforms. Future jobs in 'retail' will be very tech-savvy and very visual. It will be the norm for customers to walk through stores via virtual reality.

Overall, retailers will save billions by reducing staff. For example, in the year ending March 2018 Marks and Spencer had sales of £10.7 billion and spent £1.5 billion on employee costs, and £0.8 billion on occupancy and property maintenance costs.

The overall benefit to consumers will be an enhanced shopping experience, less environmental damage and retailer cost savings enabling goods to be more affordable and democratic.

We must also change attitudes on responsible production and consumption. What if the future of fashion was based on upcycling and accessorising versus fast-fashion which damages the environment and exploits child labour. Accessorising would be an outlet for creativity and individuality, and it could create jobs that would be compassionate and cool.

The Future Of Housing, Water And Sanitation

As robotics and technology transform retail a golden opportunity to reinvent the future of housing and community living will be presented.

Swathes of commercial land and property will become available for residential dwellings, the possibilities to regenerate living spaces are far-reaching.

The model for living will be in community hubs in locations previously dominated by shops.

Shared services and community spaces will flourish in outdoor spaces, from parks, allotments, gardens and even the roofs of buildings. Wild-flowers and trees will help to ensure that insect populations grow once again, and local production of vegetables and herbs by restaurants and residents will eliminate vegetable transportation, and increase human health and well-being.

Buildings and parks of the future could have artistry and creativity to inspire everyone. Beauty is important to all beings, even the animal kingdom responds to it. The compassionate design of cities creates positivity and can have a key impact on behaviour. For example, recent research shows significant associations between green space maintenance and deterrence of certain types of crime in Philadelphia, Baltimore, and Youngstown, Ohio. *Citylab*

What if our skylines of the future mimicked the magnificence of nature?

Technology can play a role in this, for example, projection mapping cost-effectively enables beautiful art to be beamed onto buildings, inter-nally and externally and into public spaces. Making our cities splendid will not require full rebuilding. Witness the great success of light festivals around the world.

New models of water usage and sanitation will also be needed.

UN research shows that three in ten people lack access to safely man-aged drinking water services and six in ten people don't have access to safely managed sanitation facilities. Climate change and drought will increase this pressure further. Even countries in the northern hemisphere and with advanced infrastructures will be affected.

In January 2019 the National Centres for Environmental Information reported that, "18.5 per cent of the contiguous U.S. fell in the moderate to extreme drought categories."

In March 2019 the head of the UK's Environment Agency, Sir James Bevan, announced that "England could run low on water within just 25 years."

These innovations could include household appliances that use steam and other technologies to clean and more actively embracing human and animal waste or biosolids as valuable fertilisers and fuel.

Perfect Planet Planning

Climate change is a natural process for the planet. Human contribution to climate change does need to be checked and urgently. This can be done in a variety of ways including less meat consumption, less plastic waste, less fast-fashion, recyclable tech, less full colour print as well as the imminent need for sustainable energy.

"Energy is the dominant contributor to climate change, accounting for around 60 per cent of total global greenhouse gas emissions." *UN*

With this in mind and with the world's natural resources under threat, new models of sustainable energy are essential. The reliance on Middle Eastern Oil will end. Saudi Arabia, for example, is already investing heavily in clean energy and planning on 50% of its exports to be non-oil shortly. *Canada's National Observer*

Prince Khaled bin Alwaleed and his father Prince Alwaleed bin Talal bin Abdulaziz al Saud, are both vegan, and are two of the most prominent Middle Eastern leaders investing heavily in clean energy.

But what we need in addition to clean energy is a revolution in business and life. We need to seek harmless sources of energy that work in harmony with the planet rather than damaging it, and we need to use energy wisely.

The UN Intergovernmental Panel on Climate Change warned in 2018 "We have 12 years to limit climate change catastrophe." *The Guardian.*

"It's a line in the sand and what it says to our species is that this is the moment and we must act now. This is the largest clarion bell from the science community and I hope it mobilises people and dents the mood of complacency." *Debra Roberts, a Co-Chair of the UN Working Group on Impacts. The Guardian.*

Many experts believe that it is even more urgent than this. If that isn't enough to shock us into action, the world's food supply is under threat.

"The world's capacity to produce food is being undermined by humanity's failure to protect biodiversity' according to the first UN study of the plants, animals and micro-organisms that help to put meals on our plates." *The Guardian.*

The UK Environment Secretary has warned that "The UK is 30 to 40 years away from 'the fundamental eradication of soil fertility'". *The Guardian*

Earthworms for example, are so crucial to the planet that they have been ranked the number one most influential earthly species above dinosaurs and humans. Charles Darwin considered Earthworms to be so important that he dedicated 39 years to their study. *The Conversation*

Humble worm castings (poo) fertilise soil. Worms help to mix, aerate and drain soil and in so doing help to prevent flooding and erosion. They can even help repair damaged soil, helping to fix man-made problems such as land contaminated with toxic heavy metals. *The Conversation*

What's more, "They influence carbon cycling, water infiltration, pesticide movement, greenhouse gas emissions, plant productivity, the breeding success of birds and even the susceptibility of plants to insect attack". *Dr Jackie Stroud, Natural Environment Research Council* (Nerc) *The Independent.*

Sheer human stupidity means that worms are under threat.

According to *DW*, World Wildlife Fund research has revealed that "fewer than 30 earthworms are found per square meter on intensively farmed fields. But on organic farms, where the fields are rarely ploughed, up to 450 worms live in the same area".

Meanwhile, The Independent reports that "Britain's first farmland worm survey has revealed that nearly half of English fields lack key types of earthworm."

Insects too are essential to the planet, and our very existence. Once again selfish human actions have had a very grave impact. The Journal of Biological Conservation believes that over 40% of insect species are threatened with extinction. *The Guardian*

"Insects around the world are in a crisis." *The Washington Post, The National Academy of Sciences of the United States of America.*

How many of us remember it being usual for the windscreen and front of the car to be covered in insects after a journey. How many do we see now?

"It should be of huge concern to all of us, for insects are at the heart of every food web, they pollinate the large majority of plant species, keep the soil healthy, recycle nutrients, control pests, and much more. Love them or loathe them, we humans cannot survive without insects." *Prof Dave Goulson, University of Sussex, The Guardian*

We must act now if we are to be successful, and the world of commerce is crucial in delivering the solution.

Scientists say that due to deforestation and global warming the food of the future will either have to be plant-based or insect-based.

Reversing deforestation particularly via the aggressive expansion of agribusiness is essential. We must allow each and every species of plant and animal to play their unique role in balancing ecosystems.

Ponder, for example, the special role of flowers in helping plants to reproduce via pollination and the creation and dispersion of seeds. They also provide food for insects, birds and many more, and act as medicine for all beings.

Yet we humans value flowers mostly for their beauty, grow them in intensive farming factories, often in greenhouse conditions where insects cannot reach them, and cut them off from their natural habitat - all for our pleasure. We rarely stop to consider how taking flowers from their natural habitat stops them from performing their vital function in nature.

If we are to use flowers for human enjoyment they must be grown outside in the wild, locally, in diverse varieties and without the use of pesticides. Ideally, florists would sell full plants, rather than cut flowers, and would display them outside where insects and birds could reach them.

We must not forget our oceans which cover 71% of the earth's surface and are home to 74% of all species. Up to 2.7 trillion fish are taken from the sea every year, 40% of these are discarded as by-products of fishing and 34% are used to feed farmed animals. *Kip Andersen – Seaspiracy*

It takes 1,000 gallons of water to produce just one gallon of milk, and beef has an overall water footprint of roughly 4 million gallons per ton.

By contrast, the water footprint of vegetables is about 85,000 gallons per ton. *PETA*

Agribusiness and factory farming must be replaced with modern compassionate models of horticulture.

The Future Of Transportation

Transport of goods and people is one of the key drivers for the growth in global greenhouse gas (GHG) emissions. *EEA*

Technology will have a transformational impact on transportation too. The trend for remote working will continue either from home or local community hubs, as much more business collaboration will be held in virtual reality.

Transitions in farming and agriculture and even technological advances like 3D home printing will reduce cargos and road haulage.

We will spend time more locally to home which will also help to improve communities.

All of this will help to reduce the impact of transport on the environment, something that is vitally important, but more will be needed.

If modern public transport is to be compassionate, safety, particularly for vulnerable groups, must be addressed. For example, women only carriages have become necessary in Germany in recent times after a spate of attacks. *The Daily Telegraph*

An International Transport Forum report argues that "fundamental cultural change is needed to design transport systems with women in mind. They call for urgent actions to make public space safe and secure, including infrastructure and operational improvements, public awareness campaigns, well-trained transport employees, and better reporting systems, combined with a zero tolerance approach to harassment. Some of these actions require time and resources to bring about change, but often relatively small improvements to the travel environment, such as better lighting, can be critical in changing the perception of safety and security."

In other aspects of safety, experts are divided as to whether autonomous vehicles will help to reduce road traffic accidents and deaths. We believe they could.

An urgent priority should be protecting the safety of cyclists and pedestrians. Cycling and walking are the greenest forms of transport but some of the most statistically vulnerable. Even in Holland - a country famed for looking after cyclists well - the Central Bureau of Statistics reported that more people died on a bike than in a car in 2017.

Big and small changes from mandatory cycle helmets and safety features, to more compassionate urban design are needed now.

Additionally free public transport schemes like those being tested in Luxembourg and cities such as Dunkirk and Tallinn may become modern models of the future.

Modern fuels such as hydrogen and magnetism will all have a role to play. The flying cars of the future may even run on water.

Let's be ready, personally and globally, to embrace all of the great and good Modern Models that await our discovery, and beckon us on towards a 'Compassion For All' kind of world.

The Future Of Medicine

We are all unique. Our health is determined by our inherent differences combined with our lifestyles and environment. By combining and analysing information about our genome, with other clinical and diagnostic information, patterns can be identified that can help to determine our individual risk of developing disease; detect illness earlier; and, determine the most effective interventions to help improve our health, be they medicines, lifestyle choices, or even simple changes in diet. *NHS*

TRIED AND TESTED

Dream Big

Time is a precious gift, that (in this dimension) cannot be gotten back. Be joyful and aim for the very highest outcome. Boldly and bravely manifest the best version of your compassionate plans, now!

Phrases

"The time is now!"

"Immediate Improvement."

"Our future is GOOD."

Compassion Challenge And Exercise

CHALLENGE: Seek compassionate partners who can help to manifest your modern plans.

EXERCISE: Watch the following films - Earthlings, Cowspiracy and What The Health.

CHAPTER 10
GLOBAL GOALS

GLOBAL GOALS

Principles

In an ideal world our planet would be a place for all beings to live joyfully, shoulder to shoulder, in harmony with each other, in peace and prosperity.

We have the opportunity to create compassionate cities and communities in which to live, to do business and to thrive; where prosperity is shared and opportunities are limitless and equal for all.

Freedom of thought, speech, opportunity, and religious belief, are needed, along with tolerance and understanding, to create a world in which we can all dwell together, compassionately.

Communities need to be ready to learn from and partner with the rest of the world, extending a warm helping hand of outreach to international business partners to collaborate, strengthen, prosper and build together, harmlessly.

We can pull together globally with a common cause for joint discovery - a commonwealth of learning for spirituality, science, philosophy, technology, and the creative industries.

A first step is to create equality and freedom for all - one fair law for all. Protection of freedom and democracy is paramount.

From there we can harness innovation to uphold the law, solve key global challenges and assist all beings globally.

We need to take action for the environment by implementing a worldwide animal welfare system that protects all species.

Significant wellbeing benefits can be achieved by the widespread adoption of a plant-based diet.

Medical research using new technologies such as AI can completely eliminate animal testing and deliver transformational breakthroughs in healthcare.

Here are some of our simple but powerful policies that could be implemented immediately. They were submitted to the UK government in 2016, and Whitehall in 2017.

STA - Stop Terrorist Attacks

The multiple recent terrorist attacks around the world prove that we must redouble our efforts to prevent terrorism. Many science and technology breakthroughs contributed to the ending of World War II, and as we face new threats, it is to new developments in technology and new opportunities in the political landscape that we should turn again.

Some steps to take immediately:

Tech & Security

1. Create a dedicated Stop Terrorists App for the public to report suspicious activity. Features could include:
   - it being free and anonymous to post and report information
   - a simple name, such as 'ALERT', so as to be memorable and quick to find
   - easy-to-use features such as being able to send location-tagged images or video of suspicious activity including on social media and YouTube
   - school ALERT hubs for children to share concerns with teachers about suspicious activity at home or in the community, and guidance for teachers when talking to children about this
   - could be automatically downloaded to existing phones and devices, and pre-installed on all new devices

- messages could be stored when no signal or WiFi connection is present – to be sent as soon as connectivity returns as well as receiving crowd-sourced intelligence from the public it would also issue broadcast alerts to the public, similar to the USA's AMBER Alert service or Earthquake Notification Service, and the UK FCO Twitter Alerts service.

The app could also:

2. Use the very latest artificial intelligence (AI), machine learning and predictive analytics to interrogate the data that our security forces have, far more effectively. New developments in advanced machine learning could even improve leading systems, such as the Aerospace Surveillance and Control System.
3. Scan every passport at all global ports, especially in the EU (where this is not standard practice) to feed into the bank of data that will be analysed.
4. Take advantage of new developments in the 'Internet of Things' (IoT) to install a greater number of more effective MONITORED security cameras in public places, especially where large crowds gather. We should ensure that all cameras are monitored continuously using AI.
5. Use IoT-enabled scanners and metal detectors in shopping malls, Tube stations and other public places, e.g. football stadiums and concert venues.
6. Use the best minds in technology to infiltrate, confuse and confound extremists and potential terrorist networks – a 21st century technology-driven take on World War II's Operation Starfish.
7. Update data protection and privacy laws to provide security forces with swift access to information including from social media and messaging apps that could foil terrorist attacks while ensuring privacy for citizens.

Laws & Government Measures

1. Implement a temporary ban on the sale of all live ammunition.
2. Implement stronger KYC (know your customer) regulations to clamp down on the ownership of UK companies and properties by individuals with extremist views.
3. Isolate extremists in prisons to prevent radicalisation spreading.
4. Provide free flights back to home countries for extremists and/or those at high risk, or are in the process of being radicalised, on the understanding that they will never be granted permission to return.

Influencing

1. End the practice of terrorist names being published in the press and on social media to prevent 'posthumous glorification'. French newspapers such as *Le Monde* have recently implemented this. According to industry leaders this is best practice anyway – it is just not being consistently implemented.
2. Increase the practice of high-profile religious leaders from all faiths, including the Pope, Imams, Rabbis, etc., regularly speaking out together, calling for worldwide peace.
3. Support global citizen-led campaigns for free speech, democracy and equality for all. See the recent social media campaign featuring Iranian men supporting freedom for women not to wear the hijab, or the high-profile former member of the Saudi Arabian 'religious police' now calling for moderation and women's rights.

It is time for more action. We must take this opportunity to use the new political landscape and new technology for good, and we must do it now!

SAA - Sex Abuse Prevention App

We can link globally and use technology to prevent child sexual abuse. For example, create a dedicated Sex Abuse App (SAA pronounced SAY) for the public and/or child victims to report sexual abuse or grooming of children. Features could include:

- it being free and anonymous to post and report information
- a simple name, SAA (pronounced SAY) so as to be memorable and quick to find
- easy-to-use features such as being able to send tagged information from online sources and if appropriate, photos or videos of sex abuse or grooming of children
- school ALERTS hubs for children to share concerns with teachers about suspicious activity at home or in the community, and guidance for teachers when talking to children about this
- automatic downloads to existing mobile phones, and pre-installs on all new mobile phones
- messages being stored when no signal or WiFi connection is present – to be sent as soon as connectivity returns
- receiving crowd-sourced intelligence from the public and broadcast alerts to the public, similar to the USA's AMBER Alert service
- a link to enable monitoring technology which would allow parents to detect explicit images being received or sent by children.

Win-Win On Gun Crime

Terrorist attacks in the USA and beyond, increasingly take the form of mass shootings. According to FiveThirtyEight between 2015 and 2017 "at least half of mass shootings in the USA" were terrorist attacks which was a major shift from the two years before.

Outside of the USA, at least one of every 40 people gunned down between 2002 and 2014 died in a terrorist attack. *FiveThirtyEight*

For this reason, there should be a temporary ban on the sale of live ammunition. The only people with access to live ammunition until terrorism is under control should be the Armed Forces, Police and other emergency services e.g. The Fire Department.

This solution could be a win-win for all. The "right of the people to keep and bear Arms" under the USA's Second Amendment for example, is maintained since non-lethal ammunition would still be available for purchase. It would be easier to track and prevent terrorism and the policy would have the added benefit of reducing non-terrorist related gun deaths.

Examples of non-live ammunition include rubber, wax, plastic or electric bullets and soft polymer or bean bag rounds.

There would be an amnesty period for citizens to hand in live ammunition and exchange for non-live ammunition. The live ammunition would be handed to the Armed Forces. The policy would also boost sales for gun stores due to increased demand for non-live ammunition.

According to *Centers for Disease Control and Prevention, NPR,* and *FiveThirty-Eight* more than 33,000 people are fatally shot in the USA per year.

These include:

- 21,000 suicides - more than 85% of victims are male and more than half are men aged 45 and older
- 12,000 homicides - more than half of these victims are young men, two-thirds of whom are black
- 586 unintentional firearms deaths
- police officers killed in firearm-related incidents - there were 64 in 2016 - a 56 per cent increase over 2015

With knife crime and acid attacks rising, similar temporary measures restricting the sale of other dangerous goods must be urgently introduced. In the medium term, there are also lessons to be learned from Japan which has one of the lowest gun crime rates in the world. Just six gun deaths were recorded there in 2014. Amongst other measures, the BBC reports that "Japanese police officers rarely use guns and put much greater emphasis on martial arts - all are expected to become a black belt in judo. They spend more time practising kendo (fighting with bamboo swords) than learning how to use firearms".

OFO - Opportunties For Offenders

Reoffending rates in Britain's criminal justice system remain very high at nearly 50%. The annual cost of this is estimated at £9.5 billion - £13.0 billion GBP - more than equivalent to the cost of holding the London Olympics every year. *Prison Reform Trust, GOV.UK*

The Royal Society of Arts believes that education in secure environments and beyond can help people to progress, reduces recidivism, improves chances of employment and decreases the skills gap. A report from the Justice Data Lab in 2015 analysed education in prisons funded by the Prisoners' Education Trust (PET) and found that it reduced reoffending by 25%.

We can and must do even better than this. Current prison methods are an overspill from Victorian times and are very old fashioned. Just disciplining and reprimanding isn't enough, it must be backed up with constructive ideas and re-education.

Every person has specific unique strengths and talents. New Skill-Sets should be recognised in prisons as well as schools.

Key Skill-Sets:
- academic - literature, maths, natural sciences, humanities and social sciences.
- creative - design, music, publishing, architecture, film and video, crafts, visual arts, fashion, TV and radio, advertising, literature, computer games and the performing arts.

- athletic - sports and fitness skills, coaching, sports management, and ground maintenance.
- technology - app/product design and development, augmented reality (AR), artificial intelligence (AI), virtual reality (VR), big data, coding, cyber-security, data analytics, gaming, and social media.
- languages - key world languages for modern times: English, Spanish, Mandarin, Arabic, and French.
- life skills - positive communication skills, budgeting, wellbeing and nutrition, relationship skills, meditation, all world religions, use of social media, and sex education.

Developing these Skill-Sets with prisoners should be a top priority. There should be no access to TV, computer games or mobile phones, instead, criminals must focus 100% on re-education within their Skill-Sets.

Access to mobile phones should be strictly controlled with phone blocking technology. Access to media such as TV and computer games could be stopped unless and until good performance has been delivered by each offender in developing their Skill-Sets.

To help in the Skill-Set development, books and an intranet facility for monitored study should be supplied. Physical exercise such as athletics and yoga would be encouraged for all.

Life skills would be a key part of the program. Daily meditation would take place. Before or after this, there would be a short period of 'Me Time' for every offender to do exactly what they would like, to help them discover and develop their talents so long as it was harmless to themselves and others, was safe and within the prison rules and premises.

'Me Time' would also help to change the view of being alone from a punishment to that of a happy and productive time. This is important.

Most geniuses who find inventions do so when they are on their own. It is rare that miraculous breakthroughs come in a team. Trailblazers Beatrix Potter and Greta Thunberg both spent significant time alone before they came to prominence; which may have fuelled their creative fire.

Chemical castration could be offered to all convicted rapists and paedophiles. This is castration via drugs. It reduces libido and sexual activity, it does not remove organs, nor is it a form of sterilisation and is generally considered reversible when treatment is discontinued.

A number of countries have already explored or trialled chemical castration for convicted sex offenders and paedophiles, in some cases in exchange for more lenient prison sentences. They include Argentina, Australia, Estonia, Indonesia, Israel, Poland, Moldova, Russia, South Korea and the United States where eight have permitted the use of drugs to castrate sex offenders, including California, Florida and Texas.

Chemical castration has also been trialled in the UK at HMP Whatton in Nottingham by the Prison Service and Department of Health. The pilot scheme has now been rolled out across the UK.

At least 15 repeat sex offenders in California alone have asked for surgical castration as a way of avoiding indefinite incarceration and one US sex offender, James Jenkins castrated himself with a razor blade in a Virginia prison to prevent himself from reoffending. *ABC, WashingtonPost*

The chemical castration scheme would link with other successful initiatives such as Circles UK, a not-for-profit organisation with Quaker roots. Between 2007 and 2015 in multiple UK locations it produced an 83% reduction in reoffending rates among the sex offenders it takes on after release. *The Guardian*

During their period of chemical castration, these offenders should also have access to Skill-Sets resources.

Once prisoners have been re-educated and have proven case studies (for example with testimonials and photo and video evidence) of excellence in their chosen Skill-Set, their conviction should not go against them.

Future opportunities could consist of a Second Chance Program which would work in all industries, for all Skill-Set areas and for all prisoners except those of the most violent crimes such as murder, rape and child abuse.

Those who are eligible for the Second Chance Program could also be eligible for the Universal Basic Income program if they, like other recipients, volunteered for their community.

These ideas could be implemented straight away, they could help to clean up society and address the skills gap. It is the duty of governments and nations to do our best for ALL including offenders and ex-offenders.

TRIED AND TESTED

When Taking On A Big Challenge

Relax. Close your eyes. Be still. Hush your mind and breathe. Allow peace to flow. Focus on your blessings. Have faith and trust in your higher power.

We can all make a difference with small daily or weekly actions. It can start with a daily prayer, signing a petition, supporting a campaign, or doing something for your local community. Every good action counts and may one day lead to a big step, for example, suggesting a policy idea, launching a campaign for good or even a giant leap like stepping forward to be a compassionate world leader.

Meditate On Global Good

Open your heart to life's infinite possibilities.

Know that all beings have their own unique journey. Believe in the goodness of others.

Seek and nurture the good in others.

Have faith that we all have the capacity to shape the world. Smile as you ponder the unity of all life.

Visualise your talents manifesting to benefit all beings. Be kind to others and build a beautiful world.

Your goodness has no limits, it can change the world!

Phrases

"Freedom and democracy for ALL."

"Reflect and Respect."

"Believe that we will triumph in a greater plan."

"Let's find a solution based on democracy, kindness and harmlessness."

"Be absorbed in the power of your peace."

Compassion Challenge And Exercise

CHALLENGE: Be at peace with yourself and others.

EXERCISE: Focus on your inner silence. Be tranquil.

CHAPTER 11
JUST JOY

JUST JOY

Principles

The happier you are the more powerful you become.

Joy has many benefits from improving health, to boosting business:

- "Scientific studies have been finding that happiness can make our hearts healthier, our immune systems stronger, and our lives longer." *Kira Newman, Managing Editor of Berkeley University's Greater Good Magazine*
- "Happy employees are up to 20% more productive than unhappy employees. When it comes to salespeople, happiness has an even greater impact, raising sales by 37%" *Forbes*
- "Positive emotions make us more resilient. Recent discoveries in psychology and neuroscience show happiness fuels success, not the other way around." *Action for Happiness*

Joyfulness is also catching. We all enjoy being in the company of happy people or in environments that make us feel uplifted.

How much joy do others experience by spending time in your company, your business, or with your products and services?

By being in a state of joy, we are not just helping ourselves, we are uplifting others too.

Witness the huge success of stars who focus on entertaining and uplifting the public be that through sport, music, film, TV or the arts.

If you look back at some of the most memorable and successful films and songs of all time, they are the ones which make people joyful. For example, most of the current top ten best-selling singles of all time can be considered upbeat. Pharrell Williams' song "Happy" was the most popular song in the world in the year following its release.

As a wise monk once said to Judith "Do you feel there is enough suffering in the world?" When she replied "Yes" he laughed and said, "Well, why my dear one are you choosing to add yours?"

So, going forward remember to just smile and feel the joy!

"Set your heart on doing good. Do it over and over again, And you will be filled with joy." *Siddhartha Gautama, The Buddha*

TRIED AND TESTED

Create A Joyful List

We keep lists of things that create joy and happiness for colleagues, customers, and ourselves, and actively build them into plans and schedules.

Even seemingly small things like listening to uplifting music at the start of the day or before an important activity; spending time in nature, creating an inspiring working environment with plenty of plants or inspirational quotes can make a miraculous difference.

On a larger scale, the most successful companies in the world obsessively seek to find joy-points for their customers, focusing on the tiniest details in the pursuit of excellence.

Celebrate All Good Things

In blissful joyful jubilation celebrate all that is good on this perpetually abundant planet of ours.

Start a daily practice of writing down everything that makes you happy. It could be specific things that you are happy for that day, or that you are joyful to have in your life or business. Doing this regularly will quickly change your mindset and that of those around you.

We schedule time into daily and weekly meetings to actively share success. Even five minutes at the start of a meeting to celebrate good news can have an immediate impact on the atmosphere and productivity of a team.

Create A Moaning & Complaining Free-Zone

Refuse to give in to negativity. Be a positive beacon - the answer to others' prayers. Use your energy to raise the atmosphere with good thoughts, words, and actions.

We schedule regular sessions where as a team we only focus on the good things that have occurred, and on overcoming challenges in a positive way. This could be a specific room or area in an office, or a part of the day or month that is set aside purely for celebrating or acknowledging each other joyfully.

Better still you could even declare your entire life a moaning and complaining-free zone!

Rest And Play

We aim to have at least one full day of rest every week to enjoy life and give thanks for all of our blessings. We build rest and recuperation in team time too, with generous holiday allowances, and team days which include enjoyable activities and also restorative ones like meditation or being in nature.

Phrases

"Looking forward to hearing ALL your good news!"

"Let's celebrate the celebration that is life!"

"What I enjoy about ….. is ….."

Compassion Challenge And Exercise

CHALLENGE: Sing, dance and ENJOY life!

EXERCISE: Explore ways to increase the joy of others!

CHAPTER 12
INSPIRATIONAL QUOTES

NAME	DESCRIPTION	QUOTE
GOD Allah / Yahweh Asherah	DIVINE CREATOR	"They shall not hurt, nor shall they kill in all My Holy Mountain." *Isaias 11:9*
Yeshua/Jesus Christ The Messiah	The Son of GOD.	"Thou shalt love the Lord thy GOD with all thy heart, and with all thy soul, and with all thy mind." *Matthew 22:37*
Prophet Muhammad (peace be upon him)	The Founder of Islam. The proclaimer of The Qur'ān.	"The greatest Jihad is to battle your own soul, to fight the evil within yourself."
Melchizedek	King of Salem. Priest of The Most High GOD. Teacher of Abram/Abraham.	"And Melchizedek king of Salem brought forth bread and wine: and he was the Priest of the most High GOD." *Genesis 14:18*
Siddhartha Gautama, Buddha	The Founder of Buddhism.	"Give, even if you only have a little." *Dhammapada v. 224*
John The Baptist	Prophet, Baptiser, Preacher.	"He that hath two coats, let him impart to him that hath none." *Luke 3:11*
Haile Selassie	Rastafarian Messiah. Former Emperor of Ethiopia.	"It is much easier to show compassion to animals. They are never wicked."
John The Apostle	One of the Twelve Apostles of Yeshua/Jesus.	"Let us not love in word, neither in tongue; but in deed and in truth." *1 John 3:18*
Goddess Ma'at	Goddess of truth, balance, order, harmony, law, morality, and justice.	No. 36 of the 42 Divine Principles of Ma'at: "I have not cursed anyone in thought, word or deeds."*Black History Heroes*
Mary	The Mother of Yeshua/Jesus.	"Whatsoever He (Yeshua/Jesus) saith unto you, do it." *John 2:5*
Mary Magdalene	One of Yeshua's/Jesus' Apostles.	"Now when Yeshua/Jesus was risen early the first day of the week, he appeared first to Mary Magdalene." *Mark 16:9*
Guru Nanak	The Founder of Sikhism and the first of the Sikh Gurus.	"Even Kings and Emperors with heaps of wealth and vast dominion cannot compare with an ant filled with the love of GOD." *Discover Sikhism*

NAME	DESCRIPTION	QUOTE
Ra	Ra was the ancient Egyptians' sun god.	"Egyptians believed Ra was swallowed every night by the sky goddess Nut, and reborn every morning." *AcientEgypt.co.uk*
Deborah	Prophetess, Saint, Counsellor, and Warrior of GOD. The only female judge in the Bible.	"For the LORD shall sell Sisera into the hand of a woman." *Judges 4:9*
Noah	Walked with GOD. Listened to GOD. Blessed by GOD. Unconditional covenant with GOD.	GOD said to Noah, "And I will establish my covenant with you; neither shall all flesh be cut off any more by the waters of a flood; neither shall there any more be a flood to destroy the earth." *Genesis 9:11*
Moses	Prophet to whom GOD gave the Ten Commandments.	"I have set before you life and death, blessing and cursing: therefore choose life, that both thou and thy seed may live." *Deuteronomy 30:19*
Goddess Nekhbet	Goddess of Power. Queen of Upper Egypt.	Goddess Nekhbet was referred to as "The Mother of Mothers, who hath existed from the Beginning". *Ancient Eygpt Online*
Mahavira	Tirthankara/Teacher of Jainism.	"Do not injure, abuse, oppress, enslave, insult, torment, torture, or kill any creature or living being." *Jain Scripture.*
Huldah	Prophetess and Teacher. The first person to declare certain writings to be Holy Scripture.	"Because thine heart was tender, and thou didst humble thyself before GOD... thou shalt be gathered to thy grave in peace." *2 Chronicles 34:27-28*
Krishna	Hindu God of compassion, tenderness and love.	"He who is free from hatred toward all creatures, is friendly and kind to all, is devoid of the consciousness of "I-ness" and possessiveness; is evenminded in suffering and joy, forgiving, ever contented." *The Bhagavad Gita*
Prophet Bahá'u'lláh	Founder of the Bahá'í Faith.	"Let your vision be world-embracing rather than confined to your own self."

NAME	DESCRIPTION	QUOTE
Anna	Prophetess. Anna was at The Presentation of Yeshua/Jesus as a baby at the Temple.	Anna is described in the Bible as the person "which departed not from the temple, but served GOD with fastings and prayers night and day." *Luke 2:37*
Sophia	The female personification of Divine Wisdom. Mother of the Universe.	Known in Gnosticism as one of the feminine aspects of GOD, and Holy Spirit of The Trinity.
Goddess Hestia	Virgin Goddess of hearth, home, domesticity, architecture and state.	"Zeus gave Hestia high honour instead of marriage, the richest portion, and honour in temples. Among mortals she is chief goddess." *Theoi Project*
Solomon	A blessed and wealthy King.	"The fear of the LORD is the beginning of knowledge: but fools despise wisdom and instruction." *Proverbs 1:7*
M	Cher's Spiritual Master.	"My strongest soldier and most delicate flower, let's dance the eternal dance together, forever. With GOD we can do everything."
Ray	Cher's Spiritual Teacher. An ascetic, celibate, Holy man.	"Don't listen to what people tell you. Look at their actions. Look at how they treat others - animals and people."
Madame Helena Petrovna Blavatsky	Co-Founder of The Theosophical Society.	"There is no religion higher than truth." *Theosophical Society motto.*
St. Teresa of Avila	Christian Mystic and Saint.	"Let nothing disturb you. Let nothing make you afraid. All things are passing. GOD alone never changes. Patience gains all things. If you have GOD, you will want for nothing. GOD alone suffices."
Goddess Isis	The Egyptian Goddess of Magic. Isis was a friend of the downtrodden and was blessed with powers of healing and protection.	Connected with the words: "I am what was, what is, and what will be. No mortal has yet raised my veil." *NPS.gov*
Sri Yukteswar	The Incarnation of Wisdom. The Spiritual Teacher of Paramahansa Yogananda.	"Ordinary love is selfish, darkly rooted in desires and satisfactions. Divine love is without condition."

"It is compassion that is ever transmuting the dark illusion of separateness. Its blazing light ever shining to empower the forces of good to triumph."

The Hidden Truths of a Modern Seer by Cher Chevalier

REFERENCES

INTRODUCTION AND CHAPTER 1

Marcacci, S. (2018, November 1). We Have A Decade To Prevent Dangerous Climate Change: These 10 Policies Can Limit Warming To 2°C. Forbes.

Watts, J. (2018, October 8). We have 12 years to limit climate change catastrophe, warns UN. The Guardian.

Acme. In Oxford Living Dictionaries Online.

Acme. Wikipedia.

Marcarelli, R. (2018, July 30). Plant-Based Foods See 20% Growth: Report. Winsight Grocery Business.

Richling, C. (2015, February). Plant-Based Eating: Getting the Right Nutrition. Ornish Living.

Monbiot, G. (2018, June 8). The best way to save the planet? Drop meat and dairy. The Guardian.

Commerce. Wikipedia.

Commerce. In Oxford Living Dictionaries Online.

Marcacci, S. (2018, November 1). We Have A Decade To Prevent Dangerous Climate Change: These 10 Policies Can Limit Warming To 2°C. Forbes.

Watts, J. (2018, October 8). We have 12 years to limit climate change catastrophe, warns UN. The Guardian.

United Nations: Global Issues – Ending Poverty.

United Nations: Sustainable Development Goals - Goal 2: Zero Hunger.

United Nations: Sustainable Development Goals - Goal 2: Zero Hunger.

United Nations: Global Issues - Health.

United Nations: Global Issues - Climate Change.

United Nations: Sustainable Development Goals - Goal 12: Ensure sustainable consumption and production patterns.

United Nations: World Day Against Child Labour 12 June.

Pasca Palmer, C. (2019, January). Why a healthy planet and a healthy economy go hand-in-hand. World Economic Forum Annual Meeting.

Dubbins, J. (2019, March). The Future of Food: plant, data, waste and wearables. The Drum Network.

von Massow, M. & Weersink, A. (2017, April). Less meat, more bugs in our dietary future. The Conversation.

Roger, John & McWilliams, Peter. (2001). You Can't Afford the Luxury of a Negative Thought: A Guide to Positive Thinking. London, England: HarperCollinsPublishers Limited.

Shaolin Kungfu Overview.Shaolin.org

CHAPTER 2

Austin, M.W.. (2012, June). Humility – Humility is a trait worth having. Psychology Today.

Henderson, J. (2001, July 8). The 10 greatest cheats in sporting history. The Observer.

Ashoka network of social entrepreneurs. (2012, October 2). 12 Great Quotes From Gandhi On His Birthday. Forbes.

Saints, Quotes from Blessed Mother Teresa of Calcutta, CrossroadsInitiative.com

Aristotle. Goodreads.com

Honour, Shakespeare. Wikiquote.

CHAPTER 3

Berman, J. (2014, April 20). The Three Essential Warren Buffett Quotes To Live By. Forbes.

Osborne, S. (2017, April 30). Dyslexia should be recognised as a sign of potential, says Richard Branson. Independent.

Oprah Winfrey. Wikipedia.

Mowbray, N. (2003, March 2). Oprah's path to power. The Guardian.

Miller, M. (2009, May 6). The Wealthiest Black Americans. Forbes.

Oprah Winfrey Debuts as First African-American On BusinessWeek's Annual Ranking of 'Americas Top Philanthropists'. (2004, November 19). Business Week.

Inbar, M. (2010, April 12). Biographer: Oprah called self teen 'prostitute'. Today.com.

Hamilton: I was pushed around and bullied at school. (2016, June 27). Grand Prix 24/7.com.

Lewis Hamilton. Wikipedia.

Davies, G. A. (2007, July 5). A salute to the real Lewis Hamilton. The Telegraph.

Tate, A. Why everyone from Beethoven, Goethe, Dickens, Darwin to Steve Jobs took long walks and why you should too. Canva.com.

Reisinger, D. (2019, January 10). A.I. Expert Says Automation Could Replace 40% of Jobs in 15 Years. Fortune.

Powell, T. (2017, March 24). Robots will 'take over third of British jobs in next 15 years'. London Evening Standard.

Nagesh. A. (2019, February 8). Finland basic income trial left people 'happier but jobless'. BBC News.

Earth and Space Science Units and Lessons Grades 7 - 9. Nasa.gov.

(2019, 7 March) Vol 655. Hansard. International Women's Day. House of Commons, UK Parliament.

CHAPTER 4

Bailey, M. (2014, January 22). Sports visualisation: how to imagine your way to success. The Telegraph.

Inventor Monday: Leonardo da Vinci. (2013, April 15). Davison.

Winston Churchill.Wikiquote.

The King James Bible. (2011, March 2). The Project Gutenberg EBook of the King James Bible.

Hughes-Onslow, F. The rise of Queen Elizabeth I. Britain Magazine.

Marshall, C. (2017, December 7). "Try Again. Fail Again. Fail Better": How Samuel Beckett Created the Unlikely Mantra That Inspires Entrepreneurs Today. Openculture.com.

CHAPTER 5

Four Ways Prophet Muhammad (saw) Performed Sadaqah. (2017, March 29). Muslimhands.org.uk.

The Giving Pledge - History of the Pledge. Givingpledge.org.

Hasan, M. (2012, January 2). Mehdi Hasan speaks to Muhammad Yunus, economist, on behavioural economics and his Nobel Prize win. The New Statesman.

Haden, J. (2016, December 12). 7 Things the Happiest People Do Every Single Day. Inc.com.

Practicing Gratitude Can Increase Happiness by 25%. (2007, September 10). PsyBlog.

Griffith, J. (2019, February 6). Aerosmith's Steven Tyler opens home in Tennessee for abused girls. NBCnews.com.

Lieber, R. (2010, April 30). How Much to Donate? God Knows. The New York Times.

Tithes in Judaism. Wikipedia

The King James Bible. (2011, March 2). The Project Gutenberg EBook of the King James Bible.

Chevalier, C. (2016). SLIM: Step Lightly In Mind Body Spirit. London, England: Asherah Books.

The Facts. (2016). ONS Compendium - Homicide & Refuge.

Radford, L. et al. (2011). Child abuse and neglect in the UK today. London: NSPCC.

Crime Survey of England and Wales (CSEW). (2017, March). Kantar Public, ONS.

Crime Survey of England and Wales (CSEW). (2017, March). Kantar Public, ONS.

Bentley, H., O'Hagan, O., Raff, A. & Bhatti, I. (2016). How safe are our children? London: NSPCC.

Laville, S. (2016, September 6). Violent crimes against women in England and Wales reach record high. The Telegraph.

Bentley, H., O'Hagan, O., Raff, A. & Bhatti, I. (2016). How safe are our children? NSPCC.

Increasingly everyone's business: A progress report on the police response to domestic abuse. (2015, December). Justice Inspectorates HMIC.

Violence Against Women and Girls Crime Report 2015-16. Crown Prosecution Service.

Hooton, C. (2014, June 19). Domestic violence increases 25% during England World Cup games. The Independent.

Football child abuse suspects put at more than 250. (2017, April 19). BBC News.

Steven, D. (2016). Children in Danger: Act to End Violence Against Children. UNICEF.

#YouthStats: Girls and Young Women. UN Office of the Secretary General's Envoy on Youth.

Facts and figures: Ending violence against women. (2018, November). UN Women.

Sex Trafficking. Polarisproject.org.

Puppy Farming in the UK. Naturewatch Foundation.

Tennant, J. (2016, February, 23). Cat charities estimate 4.3m kittens born in UK because owners aren't neutering their pets. International Business Times.

Neutering/Spaying Cats and Kittens (2019). National Animal Trust.

Gidda, M. (2018, January 16). The Latest Illegal Business in the U.K. Is Dog Smuggling. Newsweek.

Stray dogs still 'significant' problem in UK, says Dogs Trust. (2015, October 2). BBC News.

Grant, K. (2018, April 11). The UK's first 'cat census' has been launched to help keep the nation's nine million strays 'safe and warm'. iNews.co.uk.

Wedderburn, P. (2016, August 15). A vet's most difficult task: euthanising healthy pets. The Telegraph.

Bloodline: Tackling Dog Fighting in the Community. The League Against Cruel Sports.

Facts and Figures. (2017). RSPCA.org.uk.

Winter. S. (2017, July 18). EXPOSED: Nationwide puppy farms where dodgy dealers operate £100million black market. The Express.

The State of the World's Children - Children in war. (1996). Unicef.

Kirollos, M, Anning, C., Fylkesnes, G.K. & Denselow, J. (2018). The War on Children. Save the Children International.

Merrimen, H. (2016, October 12). Why are 10,000 migrant children missing in Europe? BBC World Service.

Missing Children Facts and Figures. Missing Children Europe.

Democratic Republic of Congo (DRC). Warchild.org.uk.

Afghanistan. Warchild.org.uk.

Child Trafficking Statistics. (2017, July 31). ArkofHopeforChildren.org.

Over 40 million people caught in modern slavery, 152 million in child labour – UN. (2017, September 19). UN News.

MacGregor, F. (2017, October 25). Rohingya girls under 10 raped while fleeing Myanmar, charity says. The Guardian.

Child Marriage. Action aid.org.uk.

United Nations: Events, Mandela Day.

From Nelson Mandela By Himself: The Authorised Book of Quotations. 90th Birthday Celebration Of Walter Sisulu, Walter Sisulu Hall, Randburg, Johannesburg, South Africa, 18 May 2002

CHAPTER 6

Black, R. (2011, August 23). Species count put at 8.7 million. BBC News.

What is pollination? USDA Forest Service.

Prosek, J. (2010, January). Beautiful Friendship. National Geographic Magazine.

Hunt, V., Layton, D & Prince, S. (2015, January). Why diversity matters. McKinsey & Company.

Covington, R. (2008, January 25). Mary Magdalene was None of the Things a Pope Claimed. US News.

Harris, E. (2017, May 17). Pope points to Mary Magdalene as an apostle of hope. Catholic News Agency.

Hill, J. (2018). Queens of Eygpt. Ancient Egypt Online.

Nefertiti Biography. (2014, April 2). Biography.com.

Guru Nanak. A brief overview of the life of Guru Nanak, the founder of the Sikh religion. (2011, October 7). BBC.co.uk.

Sikh women. (2019, April 4). Sikhiwiki.org.

Pettinger, T. (2018, February 18). Guru Nanak Biography. Biographyonline.net.

Rudgard, O. (2017, June 28). Why Bletchley Park codebreakers were encouraged to fall in love. The Telegraph.

BletchleyPark.org

Chivers, T. (2014, October 10). Could you have been a codebreaker at Bletchley Park? The Telegraph.

Bletchley Park. Wikipedia.

Copeland, J. (2012) Alan Turing: The codebreaker who saved 'millions of lives' BBC News

IUCN. (2015). The IUCN Red list of Threatened Species.

UNICEF. (2014 May). Child Labour and UNICEF in Action: Children at the Centre.

UNICEF. (2017 November). A familiar face - Violence in the lives of children and adolescents.

UN Women. Facts and figures: Ending violence against women.

Gordon, S. (2017, November 1). Global gender gap will take 100 years to close, says WEF study. FT.

Women won't have equality for 100 years - World Economic Forum. (2017, November 2). BBC News.

Thomson, A. (2018, August 15). Guys Named Dave Equal Number of Women in FTSE 100 CEO Roles. Bloomberg.

World Economic Forum. (2018). The Global Gender Gap Report.

United Nations: Sustainable Development Goals - Goal 2: Zero Hunger.

Pollard, L. (Interviewer). (2016, March 17). Newsday – Elif Şafak "across the Middle East streets belong to men" [Radio broadcast]. London, England: BBC World News.

Arpi, I. (2016, January 16). It's not only Germany that covers up mass sex attacks by migrant men... Sweden's record is shameful. The Spectator.

Legality of polygamy. Wikipedia.

Polyandry. Wikipedia.

Senn, C.Y. Ph.D., Eliasziw, M. Ph.D., Barata, P.C. Ph.D., Thurston, W.E. Ph.D., et al. (2015, June 11). Efficacy of a Sexual Assault Resistance Program for University Women. The New England Journal of Medicine.

Ha, T. (2018, June 14). We can chip away at rape culture by teaching girls emotional self-defense. Quartz at Work.

(2003-2008) Bahai International Community Reference Library, Peace 34, "The Promulgation of Universal Peace: Talks Delivered by 'Abdu'l-Bahá during His Visit to the United States and Canada in 1912

Baba Nanak. sikhwiki.org

Chahal, Devinder & Nanak, Guru. (2019). Aad Guru Granth Sahib Sacred Interfaith Scriptures.

Women in Sikhism. Wikipedia.

Baba Nanak. sikhwiki.org

Forgivness is a virtue of the brave. Goodreads.com.

CHAPTER 7

Action 6 – Look for the good in those around you. Action for Happiness.org.

Why social media can be damaging for young people. (2018, September 30). Sky News.

Haynes, S. (2018, December 18). 'A Toxic Place for Women.' A New Study Reveals the Scale of Abuse on Twitter. Time.

Troll Patrol Findings. (2017). Amnesty International.

Rampton, J. (2015, May 21). How a Mentor Can Increase the Success of Your Business. Inc.com.

Savage, M. (2019, January 26). Health secretary tells social media firms to protect children after girl's death. The Guardian.

Hinduja, S. (2018). Revenge Porn Research, Laws, and Help for Victims. Cyberbullying Research Center.

Gee. A. (2015, January 9). Who first said 'The pen is mightier than the sword'? BBC News.

Luther King Jr. M. (1963). I have a dream – Speech by the Rev. Martin Luther Kind at the "March on Washington". Washington, DC.

The King James Bible. (2011, March 2). The Project Gutenberg EBook of the King James Bible.

Annie Besant. QuotesBook.org.

CHAPTER 8

Chiorando, M. (2018, October 21). Beyond Meat Readies For IPO, Says Report. Plant Based News.

Ettinger, J. (2018, May 8). Vegan Beyond Burger Outsells Beef in Major Supermarket's Meat Case. Livekindly.

Linnane, C. (2019, January 15). Beyond Meat is going public: 5 things to know about the plant-based meat maker. MarketWatch.

Webber, J. (2018, January 23). Veganism in America Soars by 600% in Just Three Years. Livekindly.

Oberst, L. (2018, January 18). Why the Global Rise in Vegan and Plant-Based Eating Isn't A Fad (600% Increase in U.S. Vegans + Other Astounding Stats). Food Revolution Network.

Chiorando, M. (2017, June 26). Veganism Skyrockets by 600% In America To 6% Of Population, Claims Report. Plant Based News.

Webber, J. (2018, February 27). China's Meat Consumption Continues to Drop as Interest in Veganism Soars. Livekindly.

Plant protein startups vie to tap China's hungry market. (2019, March 21). Reuters.

Olingschlaeger, A. (2019, January 14). Rise of the conscious consumer: 75% of Brits adopt ethical shopping and healthier eating habits. Walnut.

Flood, Prof G. (2009, August 24). Religions - Hindu Concepts. BBC.

Religions, Karma. (2009, November 17) BBC.co.uk

Karma Quotes. Dancelightly.com

Dhammapada (Muller). wikisource.org.

1269 All that we are is the result of what we have thought. Goodreads.com

Wilson, A. Theory of Karma in Upanishads and Bhagavad-Gita. Inner Light Publishers.

Wilson, B. (2018, March 1). Yes, bacon is really killing us. The Guardian.

Monbiot, G. (2018, June 8). The best way to save the planet? Drop meat and dairy. The Guardian.

Monbiot, G. (2017, October 4). Goodbye – and good riddance – to livestock farming. The Guardian.

George Monbiot. Global 500 Roll of Honour. Global500.org.

Wareham, E. (2018, October 3). Ellsworth Wareham - 100 Year Old Heart Surgeon Still Passionate About Saving Lives. YouTube.

Davison, C. (2018, December 20). Renowned Heart Surgeon and Longtime Vegan Ellsworth Wareham Dies at 104. Forks over Knives.

Richling, C. Plant-Based Eating: Getting the Right Nutrition. Ornish Living.

Wollen, P. (2017, October 18). Philip Wollen - Most Inspiring Speech on Animal Rights! YouTube.

Murray-Ragg. N. (2018, April 27). Vegan Former VP of Citibank Philip Wollen Says Animal Rights is the World's Greatest Social Injustice Issue. Livekindly.

Springmann M, Mason-D'Croz D, Robinson S, Wiebe K, Godfray HCJ, Rayner M, et al. (2018) Health-motivated taxes on red and processed meat: A modelling study on optimal tax levels and associated health impacts. PLoS ONE 13(11) NHS.uk

Carrington, D. (2018, November 6). Taxing red meat would save many lives, research shows. The Guardian.

Number of Americans with Diabetes Projected to Double or Triple by 2050. (2010, October 22). Centers for Disease Control and Prevention.

Brooks, M. (2017, January 26). Sweet death: how the sugar industry created a global crisis. The New Statesman.

O'Connor, A. (2018, September 12). How the Sugar Industry Shifted the Blame to Fat. The New York Times.

Fox, M. (2017, November 26). Big Tobacco finally tells the truth in court-ordered ad campaign. NBC News.

Tobacco Key Facts. (2018, March 9). World Health Organisation.

Current Cigarette Smoking Among U.S. Adults Aged 18 Years and Older. (2017). Centers for Disease Control and Prevention.

Rippe, J. Angelopoulos, T. (2016, November 4). Relationship between Added Sugars Consumption and Chronic Disease Risk Factors: Current Understanding. National Center for Biotechnology Information.

(2019) Physicians Committee for Responsible Medicine, Arthritis, Reduce Arthritis Pain with a Plant-Based Diet.

Richards, J. (2018, February 11). Sir Paul McCartney, If Slaughterhouses had Glass Walls, Everyone Would be Vegetarian. Humane Decisions.

Jones, A. (2009, November 30). Sir Paul McCartney Narrates 'Glass Walls'. PETA UK.

Lomas, N. (2018). WeWork takes meat off the menu as part of environmental policy drive. TechCrunch.

The King James Bible. (2011, March 2). The Project Gutenberg EBook of the King James Bible.

Gellatley, J. (2018) Issue 70 Viva Life Magazine, Future Generations Will be Appalled by Meat Eating!

340 The greatness of a nation and its moral progress can. Quotes. goodreads.com

Pythagoras. Wikiquote.

CHAPTER 9

The Future of Jobs Report 2018. (2018). World Economic Forum.

Corvaglia, F., Cummings, J., Evans, A., Slocombe, M. (2018, July 26). National Travel Survey: England 2017. Department for Transport.

Independent Auditor's Report. (2018). Marks and Spencer Group PLC.

Spector, J. (2016, April 13). Another Reason to Love Urban Green Space: It Fights Crime. Citylab.com.

Osseiran, N. (2017, July 12). 2.1 billion people lack safe drinking water at home, more than twice as many lack safe sanitation. World Health Organisation.

State of the Climate: Drought for January 2019. (2019, February). NOAA National Centers for Environmental Information.

Gabbatiss, J. (2019, March 21). World Water Day 2019: What are the biggest water problems facing the world today? The Independent.

What is causing climate change? A natural climate cycle. The Committee on Climate Change.

United Nations: Sustainable Development Goals - Goal 7: Affordable and Clean Energy.

McSheffrey, E. & Uechi, J. (2017, February 10). Meet the vegan Saudi prince who's turning the lights on in Jordan. Canada's National Observer.

Watts, J. (2018, October 8). We have 12 years to limit climate change catastrophe, warns UN. The Guardian.

Bélanger, J. & Pilling, D. (eds.). (2019). The State of the World's Biodiversity for Food and Agriculture. FAO Commission on Genetic Resources for Food and Agriculture Assessments.

Watts, J. (2019, February 21). World's food supply under 'severe threat' from loss of biodiversity. The Guardian.

van der Zee, B. (2017, October 24). UK is 30-40 years away from 'eradication of soil fertility', warns Gove. The Guardian.

Carrington, D. (2019, February 10). Plummeting insect numbers 'threaten collapse of nature'. The Guardian

Johnson, S. (2017, March 28). Earthworms are more important than pandas (if you want to save the planet). The Conversation.

Lusher, A. (2019, February 24). Dearth of worms blamed for dramatic decline in UK songbird population. The Independent.

Jäger, K. (2017, January 30). Earthworm numbers dwindle, threatening soil health. DW.

Sanders IV, L. (2019, February 11). Over 40 percent of insect species face extinction: study. DW.

Guarino, B. (2018, October 15). 'Hyperalarming' study shows massive insect loss. The Washington Post.

von Massow, M. & Weersink, A. (2017, April). Less meat, more bugs in our dietary future. The Conversation.

Richards, J. (2018, September 25). Seaspiracy: What you should know about fish, the ocean and more. Humane Decisions.

What Can You Do to Save 219,000 Gallons of Water a Year? Peta.org.

Greenhouse gas emissions from transport. (2018, November 22). European Environment Agency.

Henderson, B. (2016, March 28). German rail operator launches women-only train carriages following sex attacks. The Telegraph.

ITF. (2018). Women's Safety and Security: A Public Transport Priority. Paris, France: OECD Publishing.

More cycling fatalities than deaths in cars. (2018, April 25). Bicycle Dutch.

More deaths among cyclists than car occupants in 2017. (2018, May 7). CBS Netherlands.

Auxenfants, M. (2019, January 29). The cost of Luxembourg's free public transport plan. BBC.com

Baldwin, E. (2018, December 24). Luxembourg Becomes First Country to Make All Public Transit Free. ArchDaily.

Colin, J. (2018, September 19). The seductive appeal of free public transport. In Movement.

Graham, E. (2016, September 7). Improving Outcomes through Personalised Medicine. NHS England, Medical Directorate, Medicines, Diagnostics and Personalised Medicine Unit. england.NHS.uk

CHAPTER 10

AMBER Alert. Wikipedia.

Earthquake Notification Service. USGS.

FCO sign up to Twitter Alerts Service. (2013, November 18). Foreign & Commenwealth Office UK.

Leonard, J. (2013, August 24). How the British film industry helped win World War II. BBC News.

Burke, J. (2016, July 28). French media's blackout on terrorists' identities is missing the point. The Guardian.

Men in Iran wear Hijab to protest the restrictive dress code for women. (2016, July 28). NowThis YouTube News Channel.

Hubbard, B. (2016, July 10). A Saudi Morals Enforcer Called for a More Liberal Islam. Then the Death Threats Began. New York Times.

Bialik, C. (2017). Instrument Of Terror: Terrorist attacks in the U.S. increasingly take the form of mass shootings. FiveThirtyEight.

Second Amendment. Cornell Law School.

Alternatives to Bullets (2015, September 23). The Marshall Project.

Non-lethal weapon. Wikipedia.

Landon, S. (2017). What Would It Take? FiveThirtyEight.

Koerth-Baker, M. (2017). What Counts As An Accident? FiveThirtyEight.

Domonoske, C. (2016, December 30). Number Of Police Officers Killed By Firearms Rose In 2016, Study Finds. NPR.

Vital Statistics Online. National Center for Health Statistics. Centers for Disease Control and Prevention.

Grierson, J. (2018, December 13). Knife crime offences rise to highest level since 2010. The Guardian

Mann, G. (2017, July 14). Acid attacks: What has led to the rise and how can they be stopped? BBC News.

Acid Throwing. Wikipedia.

The Global Rise Of Knife Crime And The Reasons Why. (2019, February 14). Body Armor News.

Japan - Gun Facts, Figures and the Law. GunPolicy.org.

Low, H. (2017, January 6). How Japan has almost eradicated gun crime. BBC World Service.

Policy paper: 2010 to 2015 government policy: reoffending and rehabilitation. (2015, May 8). Home Office, Ministry of Justice.

Prison: the Facts. (2018). Prison Reform Trust.

London 2012: UK public says £9bn Olympics worth it. (2013, July 26). BBC Sport.

Crabbe, J. (2016, September 14). Unlocking Skills Inside. RSA.

Justice Data Lab Re-offending Analysis: Prisoners Education Trust. (2015). Ministry of Justice.

Prison Safety and Reform. (2016, November). Ministry of Justice.

Beatrix Potter. Wikipedia.

Watts, G. (2019, March 11). Interview: Greta Thunberg, schoolgirl climate change warrior: 'Some people can let things go. I can't'. The Guardian.

Sengupta, S. (2019, February 18). Becoming Greta: 'Invisible Girl' to Global Climate Activist, With Bumps Along the Way. The New York Times.

Chemical Castration. Wikipedia.

Joo, Y.L. & Kang, S.C. (2013, February 28). Chemical Castration for Sexual Offenders: Physicians' Views. Journal of Korean Medical Science.

Lytton, C. (2016, May 19). Should paedophiles be chemically castrated? The Telegraph.

Sex offenders at HMP Whatton in pilot drugs trial. (2012, March 13). BBC News.

Sealey, G. (2014). Some Sex Offenders Opt for Castration. ABC News.

Rondeaux, C. (2006, July 16). Virginia debates castration as treatment for sex offenders. Washington Post.

Stanford, P. (2015, March 1). Their crimes provoke repulsion but it is our duty to rehabilitate sex offenders. The Guardian.

CHAPTER 11

Newman, K.M. (2015, July 28). Six Ways Happiness Is Good for Your Health. Greater Good Magazine.

Preston, C. Ph.D. (2017, December 13). Promoting Employee Happiness Benefits Everyone. Forbes.

10 Keys to Happier Living - Look for What's Good. Action for Happiness.

10 Keys to Happier Living - At Work. Action for Happiness.

Top 10 Best Selling Singles of All Time. Top10HQ.

IFPI publishes Digital Music Report 2015. (2015, April 14). IFPI.

Happy (From Despicable Me 2). (2013, November 21). Single by Pharrell Williams. iTunes US.

Happy (Pharrell Williams song). Wikipedia.

Real Buddha Quotes. (2015). Fake Buddha Quotes.

CHAPTER 12

God. In Oxford Living Dictionaries Online.

Names of God. Wikipedia.

Asherah. Wikipedia.

McCarthy, D. Book, T. (Producers). The Holy Bible Douay-Rheims Version, Challoner Revision The Old and New Testaments. (2011, January 11). Project Gutenberg Ebook of The Holy Bible.

Jesus of Nazareth. Wikipedia.

Yeshua. Wikipedia.

The King James Bible. (2011, March 2). The Project Gutenberg EBook of the King James Bible.

The greatest Jihad is to battle your own soul, to fight the evil within yourself. Musliminspire.com.

Catholic Encyclopedia - Melchisedech. Catholic Online.

The Buddha. (2002, October 2). BBC Online.

"Give, even if you only have a little.". (2015, April 11). Realbuddhaquotes.com.

Pruitt, S. (2019, February 22). Where is the Head of Saint John the Baptist? History.com.

Cashmore, Prof E. Haile Selassie: What was the Rastafarian messiah? BBC.co.uk.

50 Of Our Favourite Haile Selassie Quotes. (2017, May 24). Big Hive Mind.

John the Apostle. Wikipedia.

Hill, B. (2015, May 27). Maat: The Ancient Egyptian Goddess of Truth, Justice and Morality. AncientOrigins.net

Cross, V. (2015). 42 Laws of Maat Under Kemet Law. BlackHistoryHeroes.com

Mary, mother of Jesus. Wikipedia.

Mary Magdalene. Wikipedia.

Guru Nanak. (2011, October 7). BBC.co.uk.

Sikh gurus. Wikipedia.

Sri Guru Nanak Sahib Ji. DiscoverSikhism.com

Ra 'Sun'. Ancientegypt.co.uk

Deborah. Wikipedia.

Noah. Wikipedia.

Moses. (2009, July 6). BBC.co.uk.

Hill, J. (2018). Nekhbet. Ancient Egypt Online.

(2015) Nekhbet, Goddess of Egypt. LandofPyramids.org.

Mahavira. Wikipedia.

Ahimsa. (2009, September 11). BBC.co.uk.

Huldah. Wikipedia.

Krishna. Wikipedia.

Radhanath Swami on Teachings of the Bhagavad-Gita. (2011, August 8). Radhanath Swami Quotes.

Bhagavad Gita. Wikiquote.

Bahá'í Faith. Wikipedia.

Let Your Vision Be World-Embracing. (2013, March 27). Bahaiteachings.org.

Anna the Prophetess. Wikipedia.

Sophia, Goddess of Wisdom. Crystalinks.com

Sophia (Gnosticism). Wikipedia.

Hestia. Wikipedia.

Hestia. Theoi Project - Greek Mythology. Theoi.com.

Solomon. Wikipedia.

More About Theosophy and the Society. Theosophical Society in England.

Theosophy. Wikiquote.

Teresa of Avila. Wikipedia.

Prayer of Saint Teresa of Avila. EWTN Global Catholic Network.

Isis. Crystalinks.com.

Statue of Isis. US National Park Service. NPS.gov.

Swami Sri Yukteswar Giri. Ananda Sanga Worldwide. Sriyukteswar.com.

Love: Human and Divine. Self-Realization Fellowship. yogananda-srf.org

Printed in Great Britain
by Amazon